FIRST GLANCE
AT ADRIENNE VON SPEYR

HANS URS VON BALTHASAR

FIRST GLANCE
AT ADRIENNE
VON SPEYR

Translated by

ANTJE LAWRY &
SR. SERGIA ENGLUND, O.C.D.

Second Edition

IGNATIUS PRESS   SAN FRANCISCO

Title of German original:
Erster Blick auf Adrienne von Speyr
© 1968 Johannes Verlag, Einsiedeln

Cover photograph of Adrienne von Speyr
Courtesy of Johannes Verlag

Cover design by Roxanne Mei Lum

CONTENTS

PART II
STATEMENTS OF ADRIENNE VON SPEYR
ABOUT HERSELF

PART III
ADRIENNE VON SPEYR—
PRAYERS

FINAL REFLECTIONS

FOREWORD

by Adrian J. Walker

In his own foreword to *First Glance at Adrienne von Speyr*, Hans Urs von Balthasar describes the book as "an eye-witness account": written testimony to a mission that he had been privileged to accompany and guide for almost thirty years. His decision to publish this testimony in 1968, only a year after Adrienne's death, bespeaks a sense of urgency on his part, a conviction that her mission and message were vitally important for the Church. But even if the Church needed Adrienne in 1968, one might ask, does she still need her in 2016? *First Glance*, reissued here by Ignatius Press, anticipates this question with a compelling, true-to-life portrait of Adrienne in light of the mission that defined her—a mission whose reception will continue to bear fruit for the Church long after the present ecclesial moment has faded into the past.

First Glance is less about Adrienne's extraordinary personality than about the mission that shaped her into a living icon of the Church's faith. This mission was a "prophetic" (cf. Eph 4:11) one, whose purpose was, not to transmit a "private revelation", but to interpret the "public revelation" delivered once and for all to the saints. It was the same charism of interpretation that molded Adrienne's spirituality into what von Balthasar called a "mysticism of the *Word*", which found expression, *inter alia*, in an impressive body of writings capable of being appreciated on their own merits apart from any reference to their origin. It is worth stressing that von Balthasar, like Adrienne herself, unreservedly submitted her written work—along with every other aspect of her mission—to the judgment of the Church's Magisterium. Indeed, the whole point of *First Glance at Adrienne von Speyr* is to furnish both pastors and faithful with a set of resources for testing the authenticity of the prophetic charism that comes to life for us in its pages.

Adrienne's docility to the Magisterium was just one expression of an attitude that shaped her entire life as a Catholic, which began with her conversion in the year 1940. This attitude is already clearly reflected in her first book, *Handmaid of the Lord*, whose opening lines present Mary's Yes as the unifying center around which the entire existence of God's Mother takes its singular shape. For Adrienne, being Catholic meant sharing in this Marian *fiat*; it meant letting our Lady's unlimited consent shape her, the ex-Protestant, into an ecclesial soul, a living personification of the Church's fundamental act of wholehearted participation in the triune God's wholehearted self-gift to the world. To be Catholic, Adrienne came to see, was not just to acknowledge that Christ freely laid down his life for us while we were still sinners. It was not even just to acknowledge that Christ's self-gift unto death enabled us to offer him a total self-gift in response. Above and beyond all this, to be Catholic was, for Adrienne, to acknowledge that, in letting us give ourselves *to* him, Christ also lets us give ourselves *with* him *for* the world he came to save. It was this Catholic intuition that would inspire her to join von Balthasar in founding a community of consecrated people in the world, a "secular institute" devoted to contemplating Christ's Paschal Mystery as the crowning fulfillment of creation: "Everything is now complete!" (cf. Jn 19:30).

For Adrienne, medical work was a way of accompanying Christ as he returned the creation to his Father on the Cross. To be a physician meant, in her mind, to elevate the cultivation of professional excellence itself into Marian participation in Christ's sacrifice for the salvation of all. Adrienne's own form of life as a Catholic doctor, then, turns out to be an indispensable reference-point for understanding her distinctive approach to the universal scope of God's saving will (cf. *Lumen Gentium*, 16). Despite the claims of misinformed critics, Adrienne does not proclaim *apokatastasis*; she invites us to offer ourselves to and with Christ for the world's salvation—while entrusting the fruit of that offering entirely to the Father. In Adrienne's hands, "hope for all" is anything but a reduction of God's mercy to an undemanding, indiscriminate leniency; it is a costly participation in the drama of Golgotha, where God himself endured his own justice, down to the very last jot and tittle, in the very act of transcending it. This timely vision of God's glorious reconciliation of justice and mercy, truth and love is just one expression of what is, perhaps, Adrienne's greatest gift to the Church: her gentle, yet uncompromising focus on "the one thing needful", which, ever ancient and ever new, is the same "yesterday, today, and forever".

PREFACE
TO THE 1981 EDITION

This book is an eyewitness account. It describes what I experienced in twenty-seven years of close collaboration with Adrienne von Speyr. More than fifteen of those years we lived under the same roof. It is a very summary portrayal—truly just a "first glance"—based on a large collection of unpublished records. It is intended, not as publicity or propaganda, but rather as a source of objective information. I cannot prevent anyone from questioning the veracity of my statements. There will be people with a personal interest in finding them to be false, for whom "nothing can be which ought not to be." There will be many others who will at once attempt to "illuminate" the entire matter through the methods of depth psychology and so make it supposedly understandable or who will dismiss it all as completely "out-of-date" and therefore neither interesting nor credible. Finally, there will be those who will be very annoyed about a charism—should it prove to be a charism—that does not conform to the conventional trends in Christianity today. To all these persons I must say in advance that (in the sense of 1 Cor 4:1f.) their opposition does not trouble me, for, when I state the facts known to me and continue to state them in the future, I am simply doing what I must do, principally in order to present them for the appraisal of the Church, to whose judgment, of course, I submit myself in every respect.

Although at the time of Adrienne's death thirty-seven of her books were in print, and thirty-four of them available in bookstores, up to now no one has taken serious notice of her writings. No newspaper except Lucerne's *Vaterland* deemed her worthy of even a brief obituary notice. The few reviews of her books were mostly drab; no one was willing to compromise himself. At first, this surprised Adrienne slightly because, despite this reception, she was still aware of having a mission in the Church. Gradually she came to understand that during her lifetime it was her lot to talk into thin air, to work without any evident effect. As a result of this general indifference, many of those who might have known about her today do not at all and must, therefore, be introduced first of all to the fundamental principles of her mission. On the other hand, there are so many persons who knew and highly regarded, indeed, even revered, Adrienne von Speyr that the opportunity still exists to make inquiries about her life, her character, and her influence.

A word about our relationship. When, in 1940, I gave her instruction in the faith, I found that while, to be sure, she plainly did not know the things I told her, she immediately and directly recognized them as valid and true for her. For thirty-eight years she had sought them with all her might, had groped her way toward them in darkness, had prayed ceaselessly, so that the outline of Catholic truth was, as it were, hollowed out in her like the interior of a mold. A slight indication was all she needed in order to understand and accept with all her heart and in exuberant joy. In this way it may be that at that time and later, in our conversations about spiritual matters, I had some influence upon the formation of her ideas and attitudes. But even previous to her conversion and all the more after it, she had her own mysterious relationship with our holy father Ignatius (who is often designated in the following pages simply as SPN, *Sanctus Pater Noster*), from whom she learned far more than from me. I, on the other hand, was without hesitation already making use of the insights she shared with me in the first books I wrote after her conversion. *Heart of the World* (*Das Herz der Welt*, 1945), *Christ and Fear* (*Die Christ und die Angst*, 1951), *Science, Religion and Christianity* (*Die Gottesfrage des heutigen Menschen*, 1956), and so on, reflect Adrienne's earliest experiences of the Passion and of hell. She often gave me suggestions for sermons, conferences, and so on, but only rarely—and with increasing blindness, less and less often—did she read my books. On the whole I received far more from her, theologically, than she from me, though, of course, the exact proportion can never be calculated. As her confessor and spiritual director, I observed her interior life most closely, yet in twenty-seven years I never had the least doubt about the authentic mission that was hers or about the unpretentious integrity with which she lived it and communicated it to me. I not only made some of the most difficult decisions of my life—including my leaving the Jesuit Order—following her advice, but I also strove to bring my way of looking at Christian revelation into conformity with hers. If it had been otherwise, many an article in the *Essays in Theology* and, especially, the basic perspective of *The Glory of the Lord* (*Herrlichkeit*) would never have existed (though Adrienne had not the least part in their actual composition). Today, after her death, her work appears far more important to me than mine, and the publication of her still-unpublished writings takes precedence over all personal work of my own. I am convinced that when these works are made available, those who are in a position to judge will concur with me about their value and will thank God with me that he has granted such graces to the Church in our time, too.

This book contains three main sections. In the first, three subdivisions offer: (1) a short account of Adrienne's life; (2) a description of her charism and of her most important theological concerns; (3) an overview of her published and unpublished works.

The second section presents a collection of some enlightening statements that Adrienne made about herself that illuminate and vivify her exterior as well as her hidden, interior life from varying angles and that also clearly indicate where she herself put the greatest emphasis and how she herself wished to be understood.

A third section contains prayers that she herself wrote or dictated and that best reveal her spirit.

I am especially grateful to my bishop for granting, without hesitation, ecclesiastical permission for the printing of this book.

Hans Urs von Balthasar

PART I

LIFE, MISSION, AND WORK
OF ADRIENNE VON SPEYR

I

THE LIFE

THE SOURCES

Biographical information about Adrienne von Speyr can be gathered from five documentary sources:

1. An autobiography, in longhand on 284 large pages, which she wrote at my request. Regrettably this covers only her first twenty-four years. From the vantage point of a woman in her fifties, she writes about her youth, with particular regard to her spiritual development, with an astounding freshness, precision, and power of recollection. This work appeared in the fall of 1968 and is entitled *Aus meinem Leben* (translated into English as *My Early Years*).

2. A very different type of autobiography, *Das Geheimnis der Jugend* (The mystery of youth), is entirely charismatic in character. My command enabled her under obedience to recount her life from the level of consciousness of her childhood and youth. She wrote then about some of the same events, but also about other matters that she herself had completely forgotten. All were retold from the perspective she had had as a child or as a young woman. Her search for God is portrayed even more clearly in this work.

The account takes us—near its conclusion in giant steps—up to 1940, the year of her conversion.[1]

3. For the years beginning with 1940—particularly for the first decade—there are my diaries.

4. For the entire life and its meaning, there are countless specific statements of Adrienne herself. A selection of these follows later in this book.

5. Friends, relatives, acquaintances, and former patients of hers could undoubtedly add many details, and then her extensive correspondence will also need to be sorted through.

EARLY YOUTH

Adrienne put up a stubborn resistance to being born. She later thought that the suffering she caused her mother during labor was one reason for the serious tensions that existed between herself and her mother from that time until just before the latter's death. Adrienne was, and remained for decades, the unloved child. Her mother was a woman with many admirable qualities, yet it was only after her daughter had become a physician respected throughout the city and had been married, successively, to two highly reputable professors that the mother was obliged to concede that Adrienne was not a child who had turned out to be a total failure. Adrienne's unceasing kindness to her mother also contributed to winning her over completely in her last years. Yet more than once when she

---

[1] There are some insignificant discrepancies in the chronology of the two biographies that I myself am unable to adjust. They may be due to the fact that in the memory of the older woman small events are not recalled in the exact order in which they happened. Also, the second biography accentuates the interior states at the moment described rather than the temporal succession of events.

was dreaming, I heard Adrienne call out almost despairingly for her mother.

Adrienne was born at last on September 20, 1902, in the austere city of La Chaux-de-Fonds, which lies a thousand meters above sea level in Switzerland's Jura. It was here that her father, Theodor von Speyr, a native of Basel and husband of Laure Girard, had his practice as an ophthalmologist. Theodor belonged to one of Basel's oldest families and numbered among his ancestors, even before the Reformation, many an artist who cast bells or painted religious pictures or printed books. The trademark of the von Speyr foundries can still be found today among the "Bells of Basel" in cathedral towers. Later the family produced physicians and clergymen, and in each generation one finds capable businessmen. Laure Girard was the child of watchmakers and jewelers who had been very successful in Geneva and Neuenburg. Adrienne was their second child; her sister, Helen, was a good year-and-a-half older than she; her brother, Wilhelm, a physician, was born in 1905 and died in 1978; her second brother, Theodor, director of a bank in London, where he is still living, was born in 1913.

For the daily scoldings from her mother, the child Adrienne had a mysterious compensation, which she revealed for the first time in her *Geheimnis der Jugend* (Mystery of youth): a totally childlike existence in God and for God, under the guidance of "the angel" who showed her what to do and what not to do, how one prays or how one can, in all simplicity, be with God; who also instructed her from the start to recognize the meaningfulness of sacrifice and renunciation. Voluntary penance was something Adrienne practiced energetically yet without undue emphasis throughout her Protestant youth. From 1940 on, she had to subject her zeal for penance to strict obedience in order not to go entirely beyond bounds because of her love for God, for the Church and her needs, and for sinners.

There was one place where this living-in-God could also be, without interruption and almost without any need for articulation, a life-on-earth: it was with her beloved grandmother, a pious woman with a deep understanding of her granddaughter. She lived outside the city in a villa, "The Lindens", and did a great deal of sewing for the poor. With her one could, above all, just be still. Adrienne has left us a wonderful description of this closeness. The child was devoted to her dignified, taciturn father, and their relationship was one of quiet yet ever-growing mutual understanding. When still quite small, she was sometimes permitted to accompany him to the hospital to visit the sick children. The resolve to become a doctor herself, in order to help people, lived in her from earliest childhood. In her primary school years, she began to work for the poor and soon formed a society with her friends for the benefit of the poverty-stricken. In grammar school and even in the higher grades, whenever someone had broken something, she had the habit of coming forward and taking the blame and the punishment for it herself so often that the teacher no longer believed her. From her earliest childhood, she accustomed herself to accept in silence any accusations made against her. She could already read and write before beginning school and was enthusiastic about everything she learned. Occasionally she even substituted for one of her teachers who was an asthmatic. Only in religion classes were there increasing difficulties. With each new minister, new discussions arose: she felt inexplicably disappointed; the Protestantism offered to her seemed so empty to her. She insisted to her teachers that "God is different—he is not like that." As a nine-year-old, she delivered a "lecture" to her classmates about the Jesuits and the *reservatio mentalis*; the "angel" had told her that the Jesuits were people who loved Jesus totally and that the truth of God was greater than that of men, and as a result one could not always tell people everything exactly as one understands it in God. She knew nothing at all about Catholics; she just picked up various scornful and derogatory remarks about them from her environment. At the beginning of her secondary school years, she wrote an assignment about "*Les Préjugés*" (Prejudices) in which she reproached the religion teacher for not being willing to discuss other religions (meaning Catholicism principally) and accused him of putting blinders on the students. She was often sick, had all the childhood illnesses, and in addition had constant backaches that made it necessary for her to lie down for long periods. Only later was spondylitis, an inflammation of the vertebrae, discovered. She always became ill before Easter, "the angel says: because of Good Friday." On Christmas Eve, when she was six years old, she had a mysterious encounter with Saint Ignatius while walking up a steep street of La Chaux-de-Fonds. She herself describes this meeting in the second part of this book. (She showed me the exact spot later.)

For vacations, there was the "Waldau". This was the canton's huge asylum for the mentally ill located close to Bern; her uncle, Professor Wilhelm von Speyr, was director, and his sister, Aunt Jeanne, his housekeeper. Although Helen was the aunt's favorite and although everything in the house did not prove to be rosy for the young Adrienne, there was still the great garden that she loved, and her uncle soon discovered what a gift she had of calming the patients, of making contact with them, of cheering the depressed. She gave them her hand and gently stroked them. Her uncle did not hesitate to send Didi and her doll to the patients, for she did not have the slightest fear of even the most disturbed. Adrienne wished most of all to share the suffering of the ill; in her prayer, she sought ways to do so and offered herself to God for this purpose.

GYMNASIUM IN LA CHAUX-DE-FONDS

Her father allowed her—against her mother's wishes—to go to the secondary school (*Gymnasium*) because of her determination to become a doctor. She was enthusiastic about all the subjects and won two lifelong friends— Charles Wolf, later the very distinguished surgeon of La Chaux-de-Fonds (d. 1965), and Charles Henri Barbier, today director of Switzerland's Consumers' Union—the three were at the head of their class. With the minister, she debated the question of celibacy, which appeared to her to be the only correct way of life for one who dedicates his life to God and the Church. She eagerly attended meetings of the Salvation Army and there witnessed public confession of sin: this type of confession appeared fundamentally wrong to her (later, for the same reason, she also had insurmountable misgivings about Caux).[2] Her thirst for true sacramental confession would increase with the years until her conversion and probably remained the most powerful motive that finally led her to the Catholic Church. After two years, her mother managed to take her out of the *Gymnasium*, alleging that there was too much association with boys and that the physician's profession was not for women. A very unhappy Adrienne spent a year in an advanced girls' school, but she did acquire there her best friend, Madeleine Gallet. The two talked constantly about God, about a life of self-surrender; they deliberated

[2] Caux, a health resort near Montreux on Lake Geneva, was the meeting place of the World Conference for Moral Rearmament.—ED.

about how this or that classmate might be converted; they knitted and sewed for the poor as though their own lives depended on it. Madeleine explained to Adrienne: "For you there's only one thing to do: enter a convent"; but Adrienne did not even know what a convent was. One night she was surprised by her father, who found her seated at his desk, in her nightgown and chilled to the bone, studying Greek vocabulary in order to be ready for the examination to reenter the *Gymnasium*. He quizzed her and then permitted her to return there for the following school term. She was welcomed back in triumph by the boys of her class—she was the only girl among them. Her charming disposition, indomitable sense of humor, and incorruptible judgment in matters of ethics and religion made her the leader of her class.

Early one morning in November 1917, Mary appeared to her, surrounded by angels and saints (among whom Adrienne recognized Ignatius); although the angels moved and exchanged places, the whole thing had the character of a "picture", of a portent for the future—the visions after her conversion lost this tableau quality, for they became total, intimate reality. Adrienne remained kneeling at her bedside until it was time to go to school; her entire later mission was to have a deeply Marian character.

THREE YEARS OF ILLNESS

Shortly thereafter she knew: her father would soon die. He was planning to accept a professorship in Basel. Adrienne asked him: "Papa, do you think it is still worth the effort?" Her father died of a perforated stomach. Although her uncle in Bern provided very generously for the family, her mother lived from then on in great fear of running out of money and dismissed their maid. Adrienne felt that the responsibility for the family rested on her and assumed full care of the household in addition to her schoolwork—but at her mother's request, she attended a business school as well as the *Gymnasium*. She continued this work despite a steadily rising fever, until she had a complete collapse: tuberculosis in both lungs, intense pain in breathing. In the Sanatorium of Langenbruck (summer, 1918) the doctor asked her whether she wanted to know the truth. In response to her "yes", he stated that she would not live to see the following spring. She was sent to Leysin for two years; a relative by marriage, Charlotte Olivier, a very capable doctor with a practice in Lausanne, supervised her care from a distance.

Her mother seemed to have forgotten about Adrienne completely. She appeared only once in Leysin for a few hours during which she rummaged through all the drawers, read all her daughter's letters, gave her a scathing lecture, and disappeared again. Adrienne had no money and just the most necessary articles of clothing. She did some reading, Dostoyevsky above all, and learned Russian. As soon as she was allowed to be up a little, the patients from the "*Esperance*"—a convalescent home for girls founded by Charlotte Olivier—fetched her to them so that she could give them lectures. She spoke on topics like "Obedience and Freedom", "Truth and Its Degrees", "The Right to Think", "Dostoyevsky", and so on. Among her listeners was Louisa Jaques, who said to her: "You will force me to become Catholic" (something that never occurred to Adrienne herself). Louisa did become a convert, entered the Poor Clares, and died in Jerusalem with a reputation for sanctity.[3] Adrienne organized a bazaar for poor Russians

---

[3] About her: *Soeur Marie de la Trinité, Conversion, Vocation, Carnets* (1942). Translated as *The Spiritual Legacy of Sister Mary of the Holy Trinity* (Westminster, Md.: Newman Press, 1950).

who, surprised by the Revolution, were unable to return to their homeland. Pauline Lacroix, a Catholic from Paris who had become her friend, said to her: "You are made for obedience." When these two met again, years later in the Jura, where Pauline directed a home for children, the latter was disappointed that Adrienne had not yet become a convert. Adrienne once went into the unsightly and cold Catholic chapel in Leysin to pray; the tabernacle lamp spoke to her of the presence of the Lord; she knew with unshakeable certainty: here in this church I am at home in the way other people are at home in their own houses.

Barely recovered, and because with such frail health she could hardly become a doctor anymore, she decided at the close of 1920 to study nursing as a volunteer in the Deaconess Hospital in Saint-Loup in the Swiss canton of Vaud. Again she felt how foreign Protestant devotion was to her. This was accompanied by overwork, and she suffered another collapse. Only after another six-month course of treatment at the Waldau was her health finally restored completely.

GYMNASIUM IN BASEL

In the meantime, her mother and the other children had moved to Flora Street in Klein-Basel. In August 1921, Adrienne, who spoke German only haltingly, reported completely alone (her mother did not accompany her) to the secretary of the girls' *Gymnasium*, Georgine Gerhard, who later became her friend. Rector Barth admitted Adrienne for six weeks on probation (because of her illness, she had missed three years of school), but she worked so diligently that within a year and a half she was able to graduate with the others. At the same time, she took piano lessons from Director Münch, who demanded that she practice at least three hours daily. Music was for her in these years

a way to God, whom she saw more and more as "different" and who seemed not to answer her stormy prayer. A
serious quarrel with her mother carried her to the brink of
despair: Did her life still have meaning? She accomplished
nothing; seemed only to be in everybody's way. She stood
a long time on a railway bridge, looking down into the
swiftly flowing Rhine, whose waters seemed to beckon
her. Then the thought that it would be cowardly to die
won out. She lived at home like a stranger. She had one
friend: Heinrich Barth (subsequently a professor of philosophy, the brother of Karl Barth), and she was also close to
Eva Bernoulli, the daughter of Carl Albrecht Bernoulli.
In school she was the motherly counselor of many of her
classmates and was also taken into the rector's confidence.

STUDY OF MEDICINE

After her graduation, Adrienne was firmly resolved to
study medicine. Her mother had plans for her to become a
secretary in a bank in order to earn a regular salary and had
also chosen an older bank official for her to marry. Adrienne's firm resolution to be a doctor enraged her so much
that she refused to speak to her for weeks, and she forbade
the others in the family to talk with her, either. The uncle
in Bern had misgivings—ostensibly because of Adrienne's
weak health; in reality he wanted to spare his unsuspecting
niece the hard realities of this profession—so, despite her
pleading, he refused to pay her tuition. She enrolled and
then asked her friend, Georgine, to find pupils whom she
could tutor. She gave at least twenty lessons each week
until all hours of the night. She gave up her music, and did
so, in fact, deliberately, as a "sacrifice" to God for the benefit of her future patients. All the vicissitudes of her years as
a medical student will not be repeated here since she herself

describes them in very colorful detail in her two biographies. Initial dread of the dissecting sessions, which she overcame by praying for the deceased whose remains she had to study and prepare; lifelong friendships with Adolf Portmann, later a professor of zoology, and with Franz Merke, later a famous surgeon; devoted admiration for her instructor, Professor Gerhard Hotz, whose untimely death affected her deeply; the ease with which she grasped all the subjects and activities that had to do with living persons (compared to her great difficulty in anatomy); complete contentment when she could finally work with the sick, when she could make silent rounds at night in the wards in order to comfort, to help, to prepare the dying for death; her indignation when patients used in demonstrations in the lecture halls or unwed mothers in the delivery room were not treated with respect for their human dignity; her anger when a doctor, responsible for the death of a patient, put the blame on one of the nurses (Adrienne saw to it that his lectures were boycotted by the entire student body until the doctor had to give up his professorship in Basel); her admiration at the silent asceticism of a large number of the nurses. In these and many other experiences, Adrienne learned to seek the God whom she had not yet succeeded in truly finding by the way of service to neighbor.

MARRIAGE

From the day on which she had the vision of the Mother of God, Adrienne had a small wound under the left breast, over the heart. She did not reflect on it, she merely knew: it was a sign that physically she belonged to God, a wonderful, indisputable secret. Although she knew that man and woman had a mutual role in begetting a child and she was not in the least prudish—in the operating room in

Saint Loup she supported the leg of a male patient during a long operation on his genital organs and took this for granted as a most ordinary situation—still in some almost inexplicable way she remained unenlightened until her clinical semester. Her good friends were aware of this and chivalrously appointed themselves a kind of guard for her. In the summer of 1927, Adrienne, who had received a gift of money from a cousin, was able to afford a vacation for the first time. She chose San Bernardino; there she met a happy band of acquaintances from Basel, among them the editor Oeri with his family, the artist Pellegrini, and a history professor at the university, the widower Emil Dürr and his two small sons. Dürr fell in love immediately with the vivacious student, as many others had done before him. A veritable battue was organized in order to bring the two together. Although Adrienne was deeply disturbed because of her "secret", the full significance of which she had not penetrated, she gave in after a while to the pressure and accepted his proposal out of sympathy for the thoroughly good man and his children. At that time, the physical aspects of marriage were distressing and somehow strange to her, but with the years she came to love her husband so much that his sudden death in 1934 (about which, as with the death of her father, she again had foreknowledge) affected her terribly; once more she was but a few steps away from suicide. Her Catholic friend, Professor Merke, helped her over the abyss with a strong, kind hand. The couple had lived together most harmoniously. Dürr was kindness itself; they often spoke together about God. During their vacation in Italy, they went together to pray in Italian churches. Adrienne passed her state boards a year after the wedding. The family lived in the beautiful home "Auf Burg", Münsterplatz 4, high above the Rhine. Now Adrienne was left alone with the two boys, whose grandfather, Professor Adolf Baumgartner, was, surprisingly, an acquaintance of Nietzsche and, later, of Jacob Burckhardt. In 1936, Adrienne married Werner Kaegi, an assistant professor under Dürr who took over his Chair of History at the University of Basel. His multi-volume work about Jacob Burckhardt is famous. He died in 1979.

CONVERSION

Time and again Adrienne had attempted to contact a Catholic priest in order to inform herself about Catholicism at last and to express her wish to become a convert; but all her attempts failed. In the final years before 1940, she was still praying, it is true, but a deep discouragement clouded her soul. Moreover, she had discovered at the time of Emil's death that in her prayer she really could no longer attest to complete sincerity in making the petition "Thy will be done" in the Our Father. She had, to be sure, said yes to Emil's death even before it happened, but later she had a growing feeling that this "yes" had somehow been wrung from her, that she had not really given it to God in entire freedom. Because of her deep honesty, she stopped saying the Our Father; a Protestant minister made the—ill-advised—suggestion that she substitute other prayers in place of the Lord's Prayer. But in all these prayers, she constantly encountered the unpronounceable word.

About the fall of 1940 (I began serving as student chaplain in Basel at the beginning of that year), when Adrienne had returned from the hospital after a severe heart attack, we were on the terrace overlooking the Rhine, speaking about the Catholic poets Claudel and Péguy, whom I was then translating. A mutual acquaintance of ours had arranged the meeting. She gathered up enough courage to tell me that she, too, would like to become a Catholic.

Before long we were speaking about her prayer; when I showed her that our saying "Thy will be done" does not mean we offer God what we ourselves are capable of doing, but rather that we offer him our willingness to let what *he* does take over our lives and move us anywhere at will, it was as though I had inadvertently touched a light switch that at one flick turned on all the lights in the hall. Adrienne seemed to be freed from chains of restraint and was carried away on a flood of prayer as though a dam had burst. In the instructions she understood everything immediately, as though she had only—and for how long!—waited to hear exactly what I was saying in order to affirm it. She was baptized on the feast of All Saints. Two weeks later, on the feast of Saint Albert, our mutual friend, Albert Béguin, professor of French literature and later editor of the Paris review *Esprit*, was baptized with Adrienne as his godmother. Soon thereafter, when Adrienne was confirmed, Béguin was her sponsor.

Béguin, her intimate friend even after he moved to Paris, compensated somewhat for her family, who were at first shocked and estranged by her conversion. Catholic Basel did not know what to do with Adrienne von Speyr; only a few nurses at the Hospital of Saint Clare established warm relations with her. In the course of the years, new friendships were formed with Romano Guardini, Hugo Rahner, Erich Przywara, Henri de Lubac, Reinhold Schneider, Annette Kolb, and Gabriel Marcel. Slowly Adrienne's joyous and loving magnanimity was able to win back the hearts estranged from her; her mother began to visit her more often during office hours; the tensions of former years dissolved; Adrienne had constantly prayed for this reconciliation.

Her office hours, in the medical practice opened in 1931 near the Middle Bridge of the Rhine, were soon overcrowded with patients. Until the mid-fifties, when illness compelled her to limit and soon to give up the practice completely, this was the great field of her public service, which was pastoral as well as medical. She saw as many as sixty to eighty patients a day, yet each one was satisfied, and the total human situation was always considered: family circumstances, the moral outlook on life, the religious dimension when present; marriages were healed, abortions prevented (by the thousands, Adrienne once said). Unwed mothers and their children were cared for; the poor people—who were in the majority—were given free treatment. Not one office hour was cancelled, not even when Adrienne was half-dead because of her own physical suffering, which will be discussed later. In addition, many worries arose at home.

THE NEW GRACES

Immediately after her conversion, a veritable cataract of mystical graces poured over Adrienne in a seemingly chaotic storm that whirled her in all directions at once. Graces in prayer above all: she was transported beyond all vocal prayer or self-directed meditation upon God in order to be set down somewhere after an indefinite time with new understanding, new love, and new resolutions. Graces of vision: after a first and still-veiled appearance of the Mother of God, an increasingly open and intimate association with Mary, which had in it such tenderness and reverence, but also such an ingenuous familiarity, that all the "stories" Adrienne told me of Mary had an aura of something confidential about them and, at the same time, something wonderfully—inconceivably—beautiful. The association with Ignatius was no less frequent and resulted in mutual agreement and understanding that seemed truly perfect. Another, less prominent feature that I noticed in their relationship was their understanding of each other in terms of their sense of humor and brightness and their way of making light of a certain ceremonious pomp in the terrestrial church, while taking most earnestly all that concerned the service of God. Then the *turba magna* of the saints into whose circles she was drawn through "visions" and "transports" and who appeared to her individually or in groups, introducing her into the world of heaven. By means of words or in short symbolic scenes or even without words, she learned so much about the laws of the heavenly kingdom from the most diverse saints. The little Thérèse played a special role, but so, too, did the apostles and many of the Fathers of the Church and her beloved Curé d'Ars. In fact, on one occasion very soon after her conversion, as she was driving home from her office, she suddenly saw a great light in front of the car (a pedestrian also jumped aside in fear, and Adrienne stopped) and heard a voice close by which gave the key to all that was to follow: *Tu vivras au ciel et sur la terre* (You shall live in heaven and on earth).

To this were added more external charisms that operated particularly in her practice and with the sick: sudden, inexplicable cures that were the talk of the town and also came to the attention of her relatives. All this will not be discussed fully now since it is recorded in detail in the diary. Many kinds of charisms seemed somehow to be tested in rapid succession in order to achieve a particular desired result. A final point was reached when, beside the coffin of a child whose death had caused one of her friends infinite sorrow, Adrienne knew precisely: intense prayer could storm the omnipotence of God and bring back this life, but there was a higher possibility: *to renounce* miraculous power and to submit in silence to the will of God. An ever more dense veil fell over all her later works, a "Marian" veil woven out of familiar and inconspicuous commonness.

But before this, something else happened, something remarkable that terrified Adrienne. She was prepared for it (in the spring of 1941, a few months after her conversion) by an angel who stood by her bedside at night and said most earnestly: Now it will soon begin. During the following nights, she was asked for a consent that would extend itself blindly to everything that God might ordain for her. I was absent from Basel; in her letters she described to me what was happening. Now I knew that I must return. And so began the first of those "Passions", ending with the remarkable experience of Holy Saturday that was to become so characteristic of Adrienne. They were repeated from then on, year after year, revealing in ever new ways a variety of theological relationships. These Passions were not so much a vision of the historical scenes of the suffering that had taken place in Jerusalem—there were only occasional glimpses of these, as if for clarification—rather, they were an experience of the interior sufferings of Jesus in all their fullness and diversity—whole maps of suffering were filled in precisely there where no more than a blank space or a vague idea seemed to exist. Adrienne was able to describe in her own clear and penetrating words what she was experiencing—during the suffering itself, in intervening pauses, and also afterward. I have taken these Passions out of the stream of the diaries and grouped them together to form a separate book, *Kreuz und Hölle* (Cross and hell).

One year later, after Holy Week, in July 1942, the exterior stigmatization occurred under circumstances that convinced me that *authentic* stigmata, in any case, are not "psychogenic". For Adrienne, the whole situation created an intense anxiety that the condition might be noticed. (Despite the fact that her hands were kept bandaged at first, several did see the wounds, which were not large.) Even more, it caused her humiliation and shame to think that what had happened to her, a sinner, might possibly have anything to do with the Passion of the Lord. In later years, in answer to her ardent prayer, the wounds became less visible; they appeared only occasionally on the days of the Passion, but often the pain was so intense that Adrienne could hardly believe, for example, that the blood from the crown of thorns was not visible since she herself distinctly *felt* it running over her forehead. In all her experiences of the Passion, the emphasis lay on the "spiritual" sense of the salvation events, which were all, however, for her as with Christ, incarnated even to the least detail.

In the meantime—since 1943, that is—the nocturnal "introductions" to John's Gospel also began, the results of which she subsequently dictated to me. The mystical "initiation" of the first years had achieved one of the desired goals: (Marian) surrender to all that the Word of God can demand and to all it can offer to the understanding and (Ignatian) indifference impregnated with Johannine theology. The theory of mysticism that Adrienne formulated culminates in the one statement: Mysticism is a particular mission, a particular service to the Church that can only be properly carried out in a continual and complete movement away from oneself, in self-forgetfulness (she loved the word *effacement*) and virginal readiness for the Word of God. Personal states as such are of no interest and ought not to be reflected upon; all psychologizing introspection becomes without fail a deviation from the main concern—God's Word—and therefore a distortion of one's mission. This basic law is also, according to Adrienne, the principal guideline for spiritual directors.

By this time, Adrienne had been interpreting books of Holy Scripture for about a decade: after the Johannine writings, some of Paul, the Catholic Epistles, the Apocalypse, books or parts of books from the Old Testament. In later years, one could give her at random any text of Scripture with the request that she interpret it immediately; she would close her eyes for a few seconds, and then in her quiet, objective tone of voice she would begin to speak in sentences that were almost ready for publishing. She usually dictated in the afternoon after she had returned from her two-o'clock office hours and had had a cup of tea. She seldom dictated for more than half an hour per day. During vacations, she would occasionally dictate for two or three hours, but this was rare. More will be said later about one exception, regarding the commentary on the Apocalypse.

THE LATER YEARS

In 1940, Adrienne suffered a severe heart attack that kept her confined to the hospital for the entire summer. This weakness of the heart never left her, severely hindered her in work and in walking, and caused frequent, painful cramps that she was almost totally able to conceal from anyone in her presence. Soon she also contracted a serious case of diabetes and gained much weight; all movement became painfully strenuous for her. Arthritis in her joints also became so aggravated that she was hardly able to kneel. In the final years, she had absolutely no feeling left in her feet, so that when she began to lose her sight after 1964, she could no longer move about unless she was led, since her sense of touch no longer served her as guide. In the years after 1940, she would remain in bed until noon. The night was devoted almost exclusively to prayer, after

two or three hours of the evening had been spent in reading. She still read with amazing rapidity at that time, often
finishing a French novel in one evening. Later, of course,
the entire night-program was suffering, prayer, and that
"travel" of which I will speak shortly. Since the morning
hours were disturbed by the noise on the Münsterplatz
and in the house, she averaged on the whole two to three
hours of sleep.

House calls were given up since she was no longer able
to climb stairs, so, to begin with, her afternoon office hours
remained her principal time for work. But she became too
weak to drive to her office and often had to be taken there
by a friend. In 1954, the practice was moved from the
city to a newly installed office on the ground floor of her
home on Münsterplatz, but her illness was so advanced
that she was never able to work there. A very quiet life
began now; afternoons at her desk, where in hours of
silence and prayer she would embroider artistic covers—
preferably with Assisi embroidery—one after the other; or
she would—as she had done earlier in her youth—knit for
the poor and read a French book while she was at it. The
books she read were all about people and their destinies.
She read a major portion of modern French fiction: Ber-
nanos (but seldom Claudel, hardly any of Péguy), Mauriac,
and, with special predilection, Colette, whose subtle gift
for observation and precision in expression fascinated her;
all the works of feminine authors she could get a hold of
(Béatrix Beck, Clarisse Francillon, Françoise Mallet-Joris,
Louise de Vilmorin, Zoé Oldenbourg, Adrienne Mon-
nier, Anne Muré, and many others) and about whom she
lectured from time to time. She read Queffelec because of
all landscapes she loved the ocean more than any other,
especially the ocean in Brittany where we spent three
vacations; she lay for hours in her deck chair on the beach

and could not take her eyes off the play of the water, the ebb and flow, the changing light. God in nature was most present to her at the ocean; she liked the mountains less. She bought scholarly books about the ocean and prized above all the descriptions by Rachel Carson. She read Sartre and Simone de Beauvoir, Camus and Sachs, Peyrfitte and Bernardin de Saint-Pierre, as well as many detective stories. She was passionately interested in biographies and memoirs of great physicians. In these years when her ability to work was so drastically limited, reading was for her a way of keeping close to people and their questions and sufferings; something that of itself overflowed into prayer.

For her prayer was always universal, catholic: prayer for all the concerns of the Kingdom of God, and an offering of self for the needs of this Kingdom. She loved the word and the reality of "anonymity": to let one's own being be absorbed namelessly in the universal; she loved the word and the reality of "being available", an expression that appears repeatedly in her books. God took her at her word, and during the hours of prayer that filled her nights, he often allowed her to "travel" in ever new ways. Even in the final weeks of her fatal illness, she referred to having "traveled" in this way. She was "transported" in prayer to countless places where her praying, helping presence was needed: during the war, into concentration camps, then above all into convents, and here predominantly into contemplative ones where it was a matter of reawakening the spirit, revitalizing the recitation of the Divine Office or contemplation; into confessionals where either the manner of confessing was false or lukewarm or where the priest did not measure up to the need; into seminaries; often also to Rome, to the Curia, or into a very forsaken church where no one ever went to pray anymore. She hardly ever knew the name of a place, but was nearly able to describe the priest both interiorly and externally. Or she knew it was, say, a church in southern France that looked so and so. She always felt herself to be entirely and physically present there, although she herself was not usually perceived; after the spiritual exertion, she returned dead tired, for it had meant giving to the utmost of her strength in order to help as much as was needed.

Let us inquire about her spiritual reading as well. She herself will give an account of her relation to the Bible in the second part of this book. At first I gave her a variety of spiritual books to read; the letters of Saint Ignatius set her completely on fire: this was it; this fit like a glove; if it were not yet translated into French, she wanted to do it. With great love and a few minor reservations, she then translated the little Thérèse's *Story of a Soul* into German; the dialogue with her never ceased. She began the works of Saint John of the Cross, marveled at his prayer, saw it from within, but was not inclined to continue reading his descriptions of it. She also soon discontinued the great Teresa; she expressed objections to many passages in her writings. She looked briefly into Lallemant and Surin, scented their spirituality, so to speak, and made critical distinctions concerning them. She read the Rules of Saint Benedict and Saint Francis of Assisi with the greatest reverence. Other than Foucauld and a bit of Newman, I know of nothing else to mention that might have had any outside influence on her. I never saw her read a book you could actually call theological. From her visions, she knew and loved many saints about whom she had never read a line: for instance, Catherine of Siena, Elizabeth of Thuringia, Jeanne de Chantal, Hildegard, Bernadette, Anthony of Egypt, Peter Claver, Benedict Labre, John Vianney, and, again and again, John the Apostle; her dictation had begun with John, and she wished to give his spirit to her foundation.

Soon after her conversion, she already knew that, together with me, she was to found a new community (we did not at that time know anything about "secular institutes" already in existence, and it was quite a long while after it had been issued that I became aware of the Constitution *Provida Mater*, which allowed men and women to live the evangelical counsels in the world and in all secular professions open to a Christian). I offered yearly student retreats for men and often for young women as well. A few began to come to us; for us "superiors", there were years that resembled a hard school for recruits; it was a matter of recognizing vocations, of directing them; many losses and setbacks were suffered. Adrienne's investment was incredibly large, and one may hope that it will bear fruit from heaven for these communities.

Perhaps nowhere did she show outwardly her innate greatness of soul more clearly than in her almsgiving. The stories of her youth were already replete with very beautiful examples of it in which she—like the poor widow in the Gospel—was always giving away, without hesitation or concern, the last thing she owned and that she herself urgently needed. She gave much and allowed her young community to give much also, and she preferred to give anonymously. That seemed to her to be more Christlike. Nor did it matter to her if she gave to persons who certainly needed the money but often did not know how to manage it well; the joy of those who received the gifts was in itself enough for her. For years she wrote countless letters begging money for the child of an unwed friend of hers. She had anonymous letters containing money sent from all parts of the country to elderly, impoverished women, and she took childlike delight in imagining the perplexed joy of the recipients. Contemplative monasteries without means were of particular interest to her: for her they represented the Church's indispensable reserve of prayer; people should have for them the utmost concern, should provide them with the best spiritual guides, should take an active interest in them, and should strive to foster new vocations for them—she herself did so with all her might and not without success. With a very large donation, she helped a contemplative community situated in a most unhealthy section in Rome to build a new monastery in a good location outside the city.

As long as her strength lasted, she frequently gave the points for meditation in her small community; she went through the entire Gospel of Mark verse by verse (there are about one thousand pages of manuscript), then the whole of the Acts of the Apostles. For particular feasts there were special points, to which were also added many instructions about the spirit of the evangelical counsels and the specific application of these within the community.

But truly superhuman strength was demanded of her by the part she assumed in the responsibility for persuading me to leave the Jesuit Order when it became evident that it would be impossible to carry out within the framework of the Society of Jesus the mission with which we had been charged in founding the new community. Certainly I myself had more than enough proof that this mission existed and that it was to be interpreted in this and no other way. Who will deny God the possibility of expressing himself to his creature (and especially in the Church) in a way that cannot be misunderstood. For me the Society was of course a beloved homeland; the thought that one might have to "leave all" more than once in a lifetime in order to follow the Lord, even leave an Order, had never occurred to me, and struck me like a blow. Therefore, even though I had my own proof and took full responsibility for my own action—which I have never for a moment regretted since—still for Adrienne, through whom this call had come, her share of the responsibility was uncommonly difficult. A letter she wrote to my provincial at that time attests to this fact.

HER DEATH

Adrienne vehemently opposed Rilke's saying: "Lord, give every man his own death." As Christians, we should die, "not *our* death but the death given us by the Lord through the Church." "We too can entrust what is ultimate and most personal to us, the significance our death may have for humanity, to the anonymity of service in the Church. This is how we give our death for the Church."[4] Adrienne herself never set a limit to the suffering of others, their sins or their purgatory, that she took upon herself, but, besides that, she also experienced a vicarious dying that extended over decades and that, viewed physically, was inconceivably terrifying. Even in the forties there were a series of "mystical deaths" in which she had to go through the process of dying in order to live on, after returning from the outermost limit, only for the sake of a mission (once she had to die explicitly "into my mission"). She was so deathly tired from about 1950 on that I seldom asked her for dictation. Since her works numbered some sixty volumes by about 1953, it seemed to me a limit had been reached even from the standpoint of how much could be read, and I myself had accumulated as much stenographic material as I was able to handle. For Adrienne, who was penetrating ever deeper into divine truths, this curtailment which I imposed was inhibiting,

[4] *The Mystery of Death*, translated by Graham Harrison (San Francisco: Ignatius Press, 1988), 62.

really a disappointment. Her spiritual productivity knew
no limits: we could just as well have two or three times as
many texts of hers today.

From the mid-fifties on, her weakness was so great that
it was always necessary to consider the possibility of death;
no physician could understand how she could still be alive
at all. From one year to the next, the conviction grew—
the absolute rock-bottom of human endurance had been
reached. But always this point was lowered once again
to new depths. Besides the increasingly severe pain—her
body was like an organ on which all, and in fact constantly
new and unsuspected, stops of suffering had been pulled
out—there was the also increasing sense of powerlessness,
of "not being able to go on", of "excessive demand":
expressions that also repeatedly appear in her writings and
whose ultimate seriousness she now experienced. She used
to say that as long as one is still *able* to suffer one is not yet
really suffering. The "traveling" continued: here could be
seen where the strength wrung from her was flowing. At
the same time there was no diminution of the voluntary
penance in which, at the wish and direction of SPN, I had
to participate.

Four years before her final death, I was on what seemed
to me a well-deserved vacation—after having completed a
large book—when, after a few days, she telephoned me to
return (and who can estimate what the call must have cost
her, who always wanted what was best for me) since some
more vigorous practices of penance were required. More
will be said about these shortly.

It was an inconceivably protracted diminuendo, which
became ever softer and softer. A dying in the slowest
of all slow motion. She was content with it and grateful, since she was thus able to give up more than would
have been possible otherwise. In 1964, she lost her sight

almost completely; the reading and delicate embroidery ceased. She was still able to knit a little, but the more her vision was obscured, the more difficult even this became; a dropped stitch could no longer be picked up. Although she could not—or only barely—see what she wrote, she still tried very hard to write a few letters every day, above all to some women religious in Germany and France whose friendship meant a great deal to her. If the ink in her pen ran out, there were often lines and sometimes even whole pages that remained blank and were mailed all the same. The symptoms of her weakness became ever more humiliating and required constant care. As her study was on the first floor and her bedroom was on the second, she was no longer able to climb the old house's steep staircase— with its twenty-four steps—by herself, although she had struggled up it alone each evening for many years. Her iron will to get up and do something made her go downstairs every day even when it was necessary for her to be carried back upstairs each evening by two men from the hospital ambulance-corps. The last months in bed were a continuous, merciless torture, which she bore with great equanimity, always concerned about the others and constantly apologetic about causing me so much trouble. Even as a small child she had always experienced joy when it was mentioned that she might die. One of the last things she said was "*Que c'est beau de mourir!*"—"How beautiful it is to die!" For, then, God alone is ahead of us. Three days prior to her death, before losing consciousness, she once more gave thanks for everything, promised she would help from heaven, gave directions and assurances about our work on earth. She died on September 17, 1967, the feast of Saint Hildegard, whom she had always greatly revered and who, like her, had been a physician, and she was buried on her sixty-fifth birthday. Albert Schilling carved, as her tombstone, a symbol of the Trinity—the innermost center of her theology.

HER CHARACTER

Although it is difficult to distinguish between the natural and the supernatural when speaking of Adrienne's character because from her earliest years the influence of grace was so pronounced in her, the supernatural dimension in no way effaced her natural individuality: rather it underlined it. But it is one thing to see this individuality and another to describe it in words, for the magic of her personality can be expressed in almost no other way but in paradoxes and by uniting apparent extremes. At any given time, one can at first state something unequivocal about her but then be forced to complete this by adding statements to the contrary.

A foremost characteristic, which was striking from the very beginning and never disappeared, was her basic *joyousness*, her cheerful nature, her pronounced sense of humor; her appreciation of the amusing and love of surprises; always guileless, innocent, but still with the idea that only in this way can the true meaning of life, the wild adventure of existence be properly portrayed. Of course this was also, but by no means solely, a matter of having an irrepressible temperament, an interest in everything, and perpetually high spirits. (She used to say that only once in her life had she been in a bad mood, when, after driving the whole day, in the vicinity of Avignon, she was overtired physically.) On a deeper level, this was an expression of joy in God, at the wonder of his existence, his love, and her need to share her own joyousness as fully as possible with everyone else. The incessant blows that rained down upon her—not being understood at home, the succession of ever-new illnesses, later an excessive burden of cares and worries of all kinds—never robbed her for long of this cheerfulness, but they did give her a deep earnestness, a sober determination that came to be expressed on the Christian level as an increased commitment toward her fellowman and toward the concerns of God.

The second and perhaps most important characteristic was her *courage*. She did not have to struggle to acquire it, it was given to her from the first, ready to use. It can be seen over and over again in her biography; never in all her dealings with people did she learn fear. Another dimension of it can be seen in her relationship with God: saying Yes from the beginning, a priori, and without restriction, allowing herself to be led wherever he willed; this ended not only in the Cross but in hell. None of her experiences of the Passion, however, broke her courage; she always began again from the beginning and offered herself for everything, for even more. ("Ah, what terrible courage!" says Don Rodrigo about Prohèza in the final scene of Claudel's *Satin Slipper*.) What needs to be added is that she did not rush off impetuously with this courage; rather, she allowed herself to be restrained and controlled in perfect obedience to God and to her confessor. She possessed the same willingness to go forward as to stand still, where this was what she was commanded to do.

The third characteristic is that all her life she was and remained a *child*. No apparent temporal distance separated her from her physical childhood. She was full of childhood remembrances, which she always enjoyed sharing with her sister and brothers; she loved children's books and beautiful old doll-houses, which she had redecorated in order to give to other children. Moreover, she was and remained nothing but a child before God, the Church, and the confessor, with a trust that had nothing to conceal.

She possessed a specifically childlike clearsightedness for the essential character of other adults. With her childlike heart, she found access to the relationship of the eternal Son to his Father. This guileless openness of heart is probably the key to all doors of her nature and writing. This never prevented her from being a mature, intelligent, motherly woman, implacable in making demands and in creating order, where this was necessary, with traits that could almost be called manly (and that Teresa of Avila also showed to her daughters). These traits emerged when it was her responsibility to call forth obedience to God.

We must resign ourselves to such paradoxes in the character of true Christians: they mirror something of the fullness and the incomprehensibility of God.

II

THE THEOLOGICAL TASK

In order to find one's bearings in the extensive literary work of Adrienne von Speyr, which, viewed from without, resembles a forest primeval but, examined from within, possesses almost the orderliness of a French garden, it is best to: (1) proceed from the one fundamental attitude permeating the entire work and describe this, briefly, in all its dimensions; (2) indicate the place of this fundamental attitude with regard to theology and salvation history and anticipate the most important consequences resulting from it; and then (3) show how this constant center fans out into various individual fields of application that, because the experiences and perceptions granted to her were of a completely charismatic nature, cannot be "logically inferred" or deduced by any means, but were simply given in this and no other way. Nothing, however, was more repugnant to Adrienne than when, in the things of God, a system was constructed somewhere or a conceptual limit was drawn. The guidelines offered here should therefore not be misunderstood in this sense; they are intended only as points of reference from which innumerable other approaches to the work will then be possible.

1. THE FUNDAMENTAL ATTITUDE

The first separate book of Adrienne von Speyr was a Marian one. It is entitled *Handmaid of the Lord* (*Magd des Herrn*, 1948); the first chapter carries the title: "The Light of Assent", and begins with the words: "As a sheaf of grain is tied together in the middle and spreads out at either end, so Mary's life is bound together by her assent...." The *fiat* of the Mother of the Lord is the most humble thing the maiden can say or accomplish and, for that very reason, her greatest, her perfection. Since she binds herself entirely to God, she becomes entirely free in God: free for all that the eternal freedom of God ordains, and this will always be the truest, the best, and the most beautiful even should it become the most painful.

Why this beginning in Marian assent? Because Mary, in virtue of her unique election, is the only one capable of excluding from her Yes every conscious or unconscious limitation—something the sinner always includes. She is infinitely at the disposal of the Infinite. She is absolutely ready for everything, for a great deal more, therefore, than she can know, imagine, or begin to suspect. Coming from God, this Yes is the highest grace; but, coming from man, it is also the highest achievement made possible by grace: unconditional, definitive self-surrender. It is at once faith, hope, and love. It is also the original vow, out of which arises every form of definitive Christian commitment to God and in God. It is the synthesis of love and obedience—of John and Ignatius. Certainly, for John, love is shown in the obedience of the Son of God, and for Ignatius, genuine obedience is always love for Christ who has loved and chosen me; but the higher unity, the absolute identity between love and obedience is to be found in Mary, where love expresses itself in this will to be nothing other than the handmaid of the Lord. No light falls upon her, all falls upon God; no accent falls upon her assent, the entire emphasis lies upon God's Word. Pure transparency. Pure flight from self. Pure emptied space for the Incarnation of the Word, and in this state of emptiness, obedience, poverty, and virginity are all one.

The assenting person can be formed by God into the infinite: every possible figure that will be imprinted by God lies in the openness of perfect readiness. Mary can be fashioned into the Mother of Sorrows, the Woman of the Apocalypse, the Queen of Heaven. Most important, the Church can be formed from her. The perfect Church, as she should be. The Bride of the Lamb whose love for the Father made him perfectly obedient. The Church that, while time lasts, never fully attains to Mary's perfect assent but that does really possess it within herself as the inner form by which she is determined, toward which she strives as best she can. Adrienne often treated the irresolvable problem between authority and love in the Church, most beautifully in her commentary on John 20–21. This dualism, although it is not really a dualism (since love can never be only "the one side"), is the form in which the Church of redeemed sinners participates in the pre-redeemed assent of Mary, which eschatologically is to become the assent of the entire people of God. This is why in antiquity and the Middle Ages, the beautiful expression *anima ecclesiastica*, the ecclesial soul, was coined;[1] the soul freed from its egocentric isolation, broadened to the dimensions of the ecclesial (Marian) assent, and capable of being totally formed by God. The charism of Adrienne

<hr />

[1] Henri de Lubac, *Méditation sur l'Église* (1953) passim; translated by Michael Mason as *The Splendor of the Church* (San Francisco: Ignatius Press, 1986; 2nd ed., 1999).

von Speyr can be understood only from this perspective, as the following will show. It is clear from the beginning that this "mysticism" is one of pure maidenly service that any reflection upon self only diminishes. Service looks straight ahead to the task. It is therefore a radically anti-psychological, theological, salvation-historical mysticism. A mysticism that understands itself only as a charism in the service of the whole Church. It is characteristic that when Adrienne had "transmitted" some commission she had received—to her confessor, who was for her the representative of the Church—the matter was completely finished as far as she was concerned, so much so that it usually disappeared completely from her consciousness. She could not remember the contents of her books, and it would never have occurred to her to open one of them.

Mary's assent is the archetype of Christian fruitfulness. Only with man's Yes can God begin something of Christian, supernatural meaning. Only in this Yes can the Son of God become man: at that time in Mary, and now, anew, in each one who attempts to join in her assent. ("Attempt" is a favorite word of Adrienne's. A Christian can do no more than "attempt".) If this idea is taken seriously, then the truly contemplative life—as an attempt to remain entirely open for the Word of God—is not only as fruitful as the active life, but is for all Christians, contemplative as well as active, the indispensable basis of all Christian action in the world. The concept of fruitfulness is central; it expresses much greater depth than the concept of "apostolate" or, certainly, of "success". Success is sought for and attained in finite undertakings; but only the infinity of the assent that, as response to God,[2] neither anticipates anything nor knows anything in advance is fruitful.

---

[2] The German expresses beautifully the profound inner unity of man's assent (*Ja-wort*) as response (*Ant-wort*) to God.—ED.

The assent is, as we have said, a vow (at baptism the believer has already fundamentally vowed himself to God) and, therefore, a definitive decision. A Marian-ecclesial assent cannot be given with reservations, "until further notice", "temporarily", or "on a trial basis". All of existence, up to and including death, is thrown onto the scales. Here we have the key to the writings that deal with the choice of a state of life and with the teaching on the various states: *Christiane* (1947), *They Followed His Call* (*Sie folgten seinem Ruf*, 1955), *The Christian State of Life* (*Christlicher Stand*, 1956), and the many separate expositions on this same subject. They consistently and with a certain asperity pursue the teaching of two states. The serious Christian gives himself irrevocably so that he can no longer take himself back: either in an indissoluble marriage or—in the counsels—by a vow that is, as a matter of principle, equally irrevocable. There can undoubtedly be a "third state" sociologically speaking, but really not theologically. The practical intent of this entirely defensible doctrine is to bar the door to today's increasingly widespread sociological-pastoral mollifications of all definitive Christian decisions—"temporary commitment", "temporary vocation", finally "temporary marriage", "temporary celibacy". Here Adrienne remains true to the deeper intention of Loyola's *Spiritual Exercises*.

A final consequence of the theology of assent may be included in this context, although placing it here will perhaps cause surprise. The perfect, Marian assent is total transparency to God. God sees to the very bottom of the *anima ecclesiastica*, without her hiding anything whatsoever or wrapping a protective garment around herself, intentionally or unintentionally. Adrienne, the physician, had a predilection for using the expression of perfect nakedness before God. The sinner covers himself—Adam's fig leaf, the profoundly developed theology of the Fathers of

the Church regarding the "loin-cloth of animal-skins"—
but the penitent who returns to God uncovers himself: in
confession. One of Adrienne's central works is her book
Confession (*Die Beichte*, 1960). The basic thought is christological and accordingly belongs, no doubt, in the following section: just as Christ in his Passion takes upon
himself all the sins of the world and, as the Crucified—
in a confession that embraces the whole world—confesses
and brings these sins to light before the Father in order
to obtain the grace of absolution for the world on Easter,
so must the sinner as a follower of Christ "attempt" to
bring to light his own sins (which are never separable from
the sin of the world: one of Adrienne's fundamental ideas)
in personal confession before the Church, in order to participate personally and experientially in the great absolution of Easter. This thought, which is far more than a
"sudden inspiration" and which restores to confession its
often overlooked theological importance, tells us in this
present connection—which is also a Johannine one—that
sacramental confession as the self-surrender of the sinner,
without psychological reflection, in the humiliation of the
soul's nakedness, is the direct way back into transparency
to God, into the consent of the humble handmaid of the
Lord. Confession is judgment as grace (Cross as Easter),
but also grace as judgment (Easter because of the Cross).

Developing this theology of confession, Adrienne
wrote a *Traktat vom Fegfeuer* (Treatise on purgatory): one
could almost say she *suffered* it; this treatise is now part
of her "Experiential Dogmatics", which we will discuss
below. This thoroughly explicated experience of purgatory seems to me theologically richer, more differentiated
and profound, than the well-known treatise of Catherine
of Genoa. Underlying the most diverse considerations, it
is always a matter of one thing: the painful, unavoidable

experience of being-confessed by God, the removal of all hidden egoism until the moment when the soul is no longer preoccupied with its own individual salvation and existence, but only with one thing: that *God* has been offended by the sins of the world (regardless of who has committed them), and the soul would be ready to persevere in bearing pain for as long as necessary to atone for the guilt of the world: here the soul meets the crucified Savior; here it has entered into his disposition and is taken up into heaven; here it has laid aside all "original sin" and can join in the immaculate assent of the Marian Church.

2. THE THEOLOGICAL LOCUS

In the preceding pages, we began abruptly with perfect assent; this assent, however, becomes intelligible only within one all-embracing presupposition: it is a secondary response to the primary Word of God. Otherwise, perhaps Adrienne's charism would not be much more than one of those "private revelations" that today's theologians sweep under the rug with a single stroke, while explaining to the faithful that such revelations (a) are frequently dubious or simply false and (b) oblige no one to acknowledge them, since (c) everything that is essential is present in the religious doctrine of the Church anyway. But one can then only ask why time after time God nevertheless condescends to such undertakings to which the Church is to pay little or no attention. Basically, Adrienne von Speyr has already given the answer to that: *genuine* Christian and ecclesial mysticism (false ones abound) is in essence a charism,[3] which means

---

[3] Compare this thesis especially with my exposition in the commentary on Thomas Aquinas' doctrine of charisms in his *Summa Theologica* II II, questions 171–82. German-Latin edition, vol. 23 (1954), 252–464.

a service to the whole Church assigned by God (Rom 12:3–6!). And Adrienne did indeed understand her mission as a service, not, to be sure, to a peripheral outgrowth of theology, not to enlarge "side chapels" in the cathedral of existing dogma, but, on the contrary, as a service to its *central deepening and enlivening*. This begins as early as the mysticism of Saint Paul and continues uninterruptedly through the centuries as we encounter such figures as Benedict, Gregory the Great, Bernard, Tauler, Gertrude, Catherine of Siena, Ignatius, Marie de l'Incarnation, Francis de Sales, Thérèse of Lisieux, Elizabeth of the Trinity, just to name a few at random. Such charismatics were meant to set aglow the core of the faith in a new way under the promptings of the Holy Spirit. If anything in Adrienne's life and work is significant, then it is this central enlivening of Christian revelation; every one of her remarkable individual manifestations of this service—undoubtedly incomprehensible to many—receives its meaning exclusively from this center. Let us move concentrically around this theological center by way of the main perspectives that Adrienne's works suggest to us.

Obedience of the Son

The assent of the Mother is the condition prepared by God for the Incarnation of the Son of God, who wanted to be obedient to the Father for the salvation of the world, "obedient unto death, even death on a cross" (Phil 2:8), unto "Death and Hades" (Rev 6:8), so that he who "died and [is] alive for evermore" holds "the keys of Death and Hades" (Rev 1:18) because "he learned obedience" (Heb 5:8). It is through this attitude of the Son (which sums up and goes beyond all obedience since Abraham, Moses, and the prophets to the living God who commands and leads) and through nothing else that the world, which was estranged from God in "Adam's" disobedience, has been reconciled and restored to God and has become the Father's beloved creation. All of Adrienne's mysticism has its locus in christological (and thereby soteriological) obedience, which—according to ancient theological tradition—is the revelation in human form of the eternal love of the divine Son for his eternal Father, who has eternally begotten him out of love. This mysticism provides a broad biblical foundation for Ignatian obedience—which for its part had of course always been understood christologically (cf. the Meditation on the Kingdom of God in the *Exercises*). This is especially true in Adrienne's commentaries on the Scriptures, in her books about prayer, and finally in a last, closely knit work, *Das Buch vom Gehorsam* (1966; The book of obedience), which reveals Adrienne's teaching concerning readiness in all its aspects.

Thus, the obedience of Christ is, on the one hand, "interpretation" (see Jn 1:18) of heaven, of the interior life of the Trinity, and, on the other hand, the "epitome" (see Eph 1:10) of the proper attitude of all creatures before God, especially of the attitude required of the Church as Body and Bride of Christ. In her book on the theology of the sexes (*Theologie der Geschlechter*), Adrienne sets forth in great detail how the twofold yet single obedience of Christ and the Church divides itself into the antithesis of the Lord and handmaid (in Pauline terms, man and woman). The obedience of the individual member of the Church to the Church and in the Church is for her—as indeed also for Ignatius (*Rules for Thinking with the Church*)—obviously nothing but the Christian's participation in the innermost disposition of the Church in general. And, just as the Church, drawn beyond herself into the divine-human obedience of Christ, is thus confronted

with an "excessive" demand, so also is the individual
Christian required to pass beyond his personal "views"
and "opinions" (see 2 Cor 10:5) into the perspective of the
Church (where she truly obeys and her obedience is guar-
anteed). Adrienne herself was exercised in an obedience
that became more and more radical and touched all the
fibers of her soul, often in conjunction with imposed penitential exercises that we will briefly discuss later. For her,
it was a supreme grace and supreme joy to be allowed to
obey—God, Christ, the Church—regardless of the severity of what was demanded. From her experience of obedience, she was able to give the most discerning descriptions
of the obedience of Christ and also that of the Church.

Triune Life

It is in the obedience of the Son that the will of the Father
is realized on earth and the Father and his Kingdom are
present. Adrienne liked to think of the Holy Spirit as the
"Rule" of the Father that accompanied the Son on earth;
he looks toward the Spirit as the religious does toward
the Rule of his order and fills this Rule with an inner
readiness—inspired by the Spirit—which likewise corresponds to the "spirit of the Rule", indeed, is itself this
spirit. In Christ, the mystery of love's triune life is open
to us; Christian existence for Adrienne takes place within
this openness, indeed, strictly speaking, within the Trinity itself: en route from the Father to the world with the
Son, led by the Spirit; en route with the Son and the world
led home by him, to the Father, led by the Spirit. Some
readers are alarmed by the alleged "anthropomorphisms"
in Adrienne's portrayal of the relationships of the Divine
Persons to one another, by the seemingly all-too-severe
differentiation and contrast between the viewpoints of

the Persons. Certainly, all human speech about the inner-divine mystery remains inadequate, and there can always be the danger that, in the delineation of the opposition of the Persons, the unity of nature may not receive sufficient attention. But one must not forget that Adrienne proceeds from the obedience of the Son of God who humbles himself to be the "servant of Yahweh"; in fact, from the very situation where the trinitarian opposition stands out most strongly: the Mount of Olives, the Cross, the descent into hell. But it is also precisely there that the mystery of unity is definitively known in the revelation of absolute love. Adrienne cannot bring the inconceivable fullness of this love close to us in any other way than by means of a veritable kaleidoscope of "views" of this love, views that are constantly changing and yet consist of the same basic elements. Two thoughts predominate: the Cross as trinitarian event, the participation of Father and Spirit in the forsakenness of the Son. And further: the mystery of our being represented on the Cross by the Son, and how, in the future, the Father will be able to contemplate and evaluate the world solely through the Son.

Adrienne enters deeply into the trinitarian mystery through these gates of salvation history, for in it we "live and move and have our being." This "entering", however, always means "prayer" for her, because she understands the atmosphere of the triune life as sheer primordial prayer.

The World of Prayer

The World of Prayer (*Die Welt des Gebetes*, 1951), one of her larger works, begins with a bold chapter on "Prayer in the Trinity". Each Divine Person sees God in the other—God, who beyond all ultimate comprehension is the ever-greater one, eternally worthy of adoration. Thus the trinitarian "conversation" has the form of the primordial prayer, in which every prayer in the world participates, to whose "atmosphere" it must adapt; whether it be adoration, thanksgiving, or petition: the prototype for all of these is found in the trinitarian conversation. Like John and Ignatius, like Anselm and the Greek Fathers, Adrienne is overwhelmed and as though possessed by the thought that God is the "ever greater". Every concept shatters against his fullness; only the vessel of prayer carries us, beyond all concepts, on God's endless sea. Since the Son, as man, communicates with the Father in unceasing prayer, he discloses the way to the Father to the one who follows and believes in him. In fact, he uses his entire earthly existence to open to us from all sides the "gates of eternal life" (*Die Pforten des ewigen Lebens*, the title of one of her shorter works, 1953). What Adrienne experiences mystically with special intensity—the openness of heaven and earth toward each other—is not unknown to anyone who truly believes; *Gebetserfahrung* (1965 [Experience of prayer]), from which a great deal is learned about Adrienne's intimate prayer life, shows that frequently the transitions between "ordinary" and "mystical" prayer are fluid; this is, as we know, in accord with the Fathers' and Aquinas' teaching about the "gifts of the Holy Spirit", which, in a supernatural way, permeate the life and prayer of every living Christian who is obedient to God the Spirit. That there are so many ways to enter heaven from earth, that the "beyond" is not far from us but fully present, is, for our time, an especially significant message.

It is for man a matter of encountering the living God in his life and of withstanding the shock of this encounter. He must allow himself to be taken by God (again in his fundamental consent) and to be sheltered by him; he must allow the Word of God to predominate over his own truth; and he must allow himself, with all his worldly dealings and cares, to be responsive to God. Only then is he living in prayer, in joy, and in truth. That is the theme of the book *Man before God* (*Der Mensch vor Gott*, 1966).

But there is no equilibrium between man and God that can be attained once and for all. Man must always let himself be surprised, disarmed, conquered anew by God. And the more he experiences and learns to understand the immeasurable love of God, the greater will the demands of this love appear to him in his life. The small book *The Boundless God* (*Der grenzenlose Gott*, 1955) shows, however, how little man is abandoned and lost in his surrender to God, how much God the Father, in the Incarnate Son and in the guidance of the Holy Spirit, prepares the way for man's access to himself and allows him to be at home in his divine world.

In *The Face of the Father* (*Das Angesicht des Vaters*, 1955), the heavenly dimension of the trinitarian perspective is developed. Adrienne's teaching is not christocentric in the sense that she does not continuously recognize in Christ, as in the Spirit, a reference to the ultimate origin of love: the Father. In her treatise on mystical prayer (see below), she depicts a special form of visions, which she calls the "Father visions"—of course not a figure-like vision of the Father, but rather a being permitted to enter into the perspective and special atmosphere of the Father. All of Adrienne's mysticism is thoroughly trinitarian, without her ever having formulated an abstract doctrine of the Trinity. Together with John and Paul, she takes every opportunity to advance from the concept of the Trinity as disclosed in salvation history (economic Trinity) to the region of the eternally personal love, always only in prayer, of course. Even all of her exegetical commentaries were for her a form of contemplative prayer.

The Mystery of Holy Saturday

Within Adrienne's broader theological position, there remains to be discussed what I consider to be the greatest theological gift she received from God and left to the Church. From 1941 on, year after year—in the interior experiences that she has described—she was allowed to share in the suffering of Christ. This occurred during the days of Holy Week (and often the whole of Lent was an intensive preparation for it). A landscape of pain of undreamt-of variety was disclosed to me, who was permitted to assist her: how many and diverse were the kinds of fear, at the Mount of Olives and at the Cross, how many kinds of shame, outrage, and humiliation, how many forms of Godforsakenness, of Christ's relation to the sin of the world, quite apart from the inexhaustible abundance of physical pain. Christ's Passion, viewed from within, is of a diversity that the biblical texts and images leave hidden; but numerous mystics through the centuries have been allowed to experience a great deal of it in ever-varying aspects—if only by drops, as it were, compared with the Son of God. In Adrienne's Passions, it was the vagueness of the relation of her own sufferings to those of the Lord that was particularly impressive. While she was experiencing the weight of sins upon herself, she knew herself to be an inveterate sinner, separated by an abyss from the purity of the Lamb of God, and yet in an inconceivable proximity to him. A basic shyness and reverence prevented her from conceiving of this feeling of proximity even as a discreet form of participation, let alone as "identity".

Each year the Passion ended on Good Friday, at about three o'clock in the afternoon, with a deathlike trance into which flashed the thrust of the lance. Then, shortly thereafter, began the "descent into hell" (which lasted into the early morning hours of Easter Sunday) about which Adrienne gave detailed accounts year after year. It was here, by the way, that her eminent gift for precise and full formulation was decisively important. These descriptions, which are always similar and yet each time introduce a variation of the theme, circling around the profound mystery from all sides, have been collected in volume 3 of her posthumous works (*Nachlasswerke*) under the title *Kreuz und Hölle I* (Cross and hell, I); only the main theme can be outlined with a few words here. It is Christ's final act of obedience toward his Father that he descends "into hell" (or "underworld", Hades, Sheol). Because hell is (already in the Old Covenant) the place where God is absent, where there is no longer the light of faith, hope, love, of participation in God's life; hell is what the judging God condemned and cast out of his creation; it is filled with all that is irreconcilable with God, from which he turns away for all eternity. It is filled with the reality of all the world's godlessness, with the sum of the world's sin; therefore, with precisely all of that from which the Crucified has freed the world. In hell he encounters his own work of salvation, not in Easter triumph, but in the uttermost night of obedience, truly the "obedience of a corpse". He encounters the horror of sin separated from men. He "walks" through sin (without leaving a trace, since, in hell and in death, there is neither time nor direction); and, traversing its formlessness, he experiences the second chaos. While bereft of any spiritual light emanating from the Father, in sheer obedience, he must seek the Father where he cannot find him under any circumstances. And yet, this hell is a final mystery of the Father as the Creator (who made allowances for the freedom of man). And so, in this darkness, the Incarnate Son learns "experientially" what until then was "reserved" for the Father. Hell, seen in this way, is, in its *final* possibility, a trinitarian event. On Good Friday, the Father hands the "key" to it over to the Son.

These remarks are only intended to give a first impression; they certainly do not exhaust the wealth of this theology of Holy Saturday. What Adrienne experienced is actually more horrible than the hell depicted for us by medieval imagination; it is the knowledge of having lost God forever; it is being engulfed in the chaotic mire of the anti-divine; the absence of faith, hope, and love; the loss as well, therefore, of any human communication. It is the metamorphosis of thought into a meaningless prattle of lifeless logic. Her experience of it was so real that, in view of it, it would be ridiculous and blasphemous to speak of the nonexistence of hell or even just of *apokatastasis* in the "systematic" sense. Adrienne's experience is unique in the history of theology; it moves us beyond the Either/ Or of Origen and Augustine. It justifies the exaltation of Christian hope over fear and yet, through its trinitarian interpretation, gives the whole problem an altogether *Christian* seriousness, perhaps never before known.

One final remark: during the year Adrienne also frequently experienced states that could be called "missions of hell" [*Auftragshöllen*], the records of which I have collected in an extensive volume, *Kreuz und Hölle II* (Cross and hell, II). These states were transports (ecstasies) into a hell-like condition of absolute objectivity of obedience to the mission and to what was to be transmitted. Afterward she usually recalled nothing of what had transpired. I was able to restore these memories to her under obedience, however, so that she might explain them to me more fully. In these states, she was no longer the loving woman, but the mere vehicle of a truth that had to be communicated or explained; she no longer recognized me. I was merely someone who was present to learn something and who understood nothing to begin with, which often caused her to make sarcastic remarks (for so much stupidity in divine matters). Finally, she would give some sort of signal that the lesson was over; then she was to return to her "normal" state of consciousness by means of a simple prayer together. These "missions of hell" were, as it were, extensions of Holy Saturday's central mystery of obedience and are therefore mentioned here.

3. THE CHARISMATIC GIFTS

The things that remain to be described in what follows are only emanations from and modes of application of the center that has been pointed out. They differ in part from the preceding in that in relation to the charismatic gifts of the past centuries of the Church, there is something unique, something exceptional about Adrienne's. But this has more to do with the path taken than with the aspired goal, which has always been the enlivening of faith, the existentialization of dogma, the radicalization of a consistent Christian attitude. And Adrienne's obedience—which determines and is the basis for everything here—was certainly, in its extent and modes of application, completely rooted in grace. Yet her obedience, as total readiness, can also serve as an ideal toward which even we who are imperfect can strive, even if it is never attainable in the same way. In reading the following, it should be remembered that true charisms are a gift from God and can (despite 1 Cor 12:31a) by no means be attained or even striven for through some sort of spiritual training.[4] The center of everything was and remained Marian assent, which we

---

[4] We are not talking here about the bond with God that is accessible to all Christians who are seriously seeking and is to be pursued by them. This is bestowed through the "gifts of the Holy Spirit" and can lead to a certain "experience" of God in prayer. Without serious penance and renunciation, however, no one can arrive at an enlivening of faith, hope, and love.

have described as the renunciation of any limit in placing oneself at God's disposal. The intention of these missions was to expand this assent in Adrienne, to plumb its depth, to bring it into an ever-greater plasticity, and to show forth God's unlimited possibilities of dealing with the assenting soul according to his will and simultaneously to show the absolute fruitfulness of this readiness.

Ecclesiastical Obedience and Authority

This presupposed that the representative of the Church had an authority to command that was not limited in a qualitative sense, for Christian obedience cannot consist in a dualism between obedience to God and obedience to the Church where the Church is really the visible representation of Christ in the world. But since it is obvious that an individual confessor does not represent the fullness of the ecclesiastical office, nor is there a guarantee that he can represent God's pure will in each direction he gives—which, however, was precisely what was necessary in this unique charismatic case—the following way was chosen to achieve absolute ecclesiastical obedience: Adrienne was able to "transmit" instructions from heaven in total disinterestedness and without any personal curiosity and could forget them under obedience just as completely. She transmitted to me—as the representative of authority—a complete and often very varied and complicated "program", which was mainly concerned with penitential exercises. "Under obedience", she would forget it completely, and I was obliged to impose the program "with authority" (a penance for me, since I would have much rather done the penance myself than demand it from her). This again was done in such exacting obedience that at times I had to start all over again when, through inattention or negligence, I had made a mistake. I was treated like a schoolboy by SPN: I had to learn that one can only command if one is under strict obedience oneself. As part of the "program", moreover, it was often necessary for me to turn myself into "sheer authority" in my behavior toward Adrienne. Every "dialogue-situation" was excluded—by a corresponding agreement of Adrienne's soul—so that it became experientially clear that the obedience of the Church can and at times must have all the reality and the relentlessness of the Cross itself, both in the authority that commands and in the faithful who obey. This, however, concerned only the particularly "grave situation", for it also happened that the other "exercises" were to be executed in the spirit and manner of personal love. In either case, of course, not according to a whim but in obedience. In many places in Adrienne's work, the idea recurs that the Christian should let his response be determined by God and by what God requires at any given moment. For example, his own personal sadness on Easter must not prevent him from being joyful *in the Lord*. For "whether we live or whether we die, we are the Lord's" (Rom 14:8), so as to live with *him* and die with *him* according to his will. Each time these bitter "programs of penance" (practices throughout twenty-five years) could last for several days. Yet each time, they produced an unexpected sweet fruit as they were subsequently interpreted in connection with some mystery of faith, and something most profound and deeply enriching was brought to light in this way. We had been working toward this without suspecting it. And the extreme "discomfort" of sheer authority, with respect to both commanding and obeying—which was often enough connected with the feeling of excessive demand—was (only now, in retrospect) revealed in its closeness to the Cross. Obviously my "role" in this "play before God" was infinitely easier than that of Adrienne, who always had to preserve absolute interior willingness, readiness, availability for any mission—however adverse—as an inner attitude. A twofold consequence of these exercises in obedience entered into her works: first, there are those aspects which refer to the ecclesiastical and general Christian obedience; secondly, there are those "fruits" which were picked from them for the understanding of the mysteries of revelation.

The Prayers of the Saints

Adrienne's mission for the Church of today is essentially one of revitalizing (personal as well as community) prayer. A particularly beautiful part of her mission consisted in making the "World of Prayer" come alive for us not only in abstract phrases but in concrete images. Insight into the prayer life of numerous saints was granted to Adrienne. That her conversion occurred on All Saints' Day was deeply significant. She once called the saints the "train of the Mother of God", which means, more precisely, that all holiness and all prayer of the saints radiate from the innermost center of Marian-ecclesial assent to the Word of God.

It was Adrienne's special, anonymous, total availability—the greatest gift of grace bestowed on her—that permitted her *anima ecclesiastica*, in the communion of saints, to put herself in the place of individual saints or other faithful in order to see and describe their prayer, their whole attitude before God, from this interior viewpoint. This was obviously possible only with those who were dead, for as long as people were alive, they were still free to change their relationship to God; it could not be viewed as a whole. For a full appreciation of this extraordinary charism, the factor of "confession"—or, with regard to heaven, that of being completely transparent to one another—must again be considered.[5] For, measured with respect to absolute assent, not all the "saints" appear by any means to be equally holy. Quite apart from the fact that some (certain stigmatics, for example), who were, of course, not canonized but who were considered from a distance as being fairly holy, were imposters. Several such cases are described. No, even true saints often have faults. These already emerged in the portraits in the first volume of *The Book of All Saints* (*Das Allerheiligenbuch*). They were still more accurately illuminated when Adrienne was obliged to test the degree of readiness of various saints under obedience (in the second volume of *The Book of All Saints*). The factor of "confession" is of significance here insofar as the unveiling of perfection is more important than the covering up of imperfection, and, therefore, the saints in heaven do not hesitate to bring some of their former opacities to light as a contribution to the Church's total transparency to Christ. But this is incidental compared to the overwhelming abundance of light and—what may be the most striking in these approximately 250 portraits—the astonishing diversity of forms of prayer. (For it is *only* with this that we are concerned in these portraits, not, for instance, with the saints' achievements in theology or other areas, where such are present.) Nowhere is there a cliché, a commonplace, a repetition. A brief, but unmistakable, portrait is sketched for each of them.

At first it was the case that at night during her hours of prayer, Adrienne would see a saint who would show her his attitude of prayer; she would tell me about this

---

[5] For the sake of completeness, another factor should be mentioned here, one that will be explained later when we talk about the commentary on the Book of Revelation: namely, the theological possibility of an "observation post", from which the visionary follows the events of the Apocalypse.

within the next few days, and I would write it down. She would not always know the exact name of the saint. Once she said to me, "Last night I saw Gregory." I asked her, "Which Gregory?" This she did not know. From her description it became absolutely clear that it was Gregory Nazianzen, as any patristics scholar would confirm. Later, even during the daytime while we were working, I could ask her for any saint. Thus the selection of figures was largely determined by me—there are even uncanonized saints among them, great artists, kings, a few Protestants. A short prayer would "transport" Adrienne into the "ecstasy of obedience"; a short prayer would bring her back to this world at the end. Everything took place in the greatest tranquility and decorum. Between two such accounts, she was able to take care of telephone purchases, have tea, receive visitors, and so on. Moreover, it was possible to ask supplementary questions, even during the ecstasy itself, after Adrienne had concluded her description, and the questions were answered.

A great number of portraits emerged that were totally different from what I had expected. Often I had not expected anything since I knew hardly more than the name of those whom I had requested. Or I had read, for example, in the theologically very inadequate book by Herbert Thurston about *Accompanying Physical Phenomena in Mysticism* (1956), the account of some events in the life of Maria de la Visitación (b. 1541 in Lisbon)—who was completely unknown to me. But the portrait drawn by Thurston (who hastily dismisses her as a "religious imposter") did not seem to me to be even partially convincing. I questioned Adrienne, and she sketched an interior portrait for me that put everything in its right place and made it completely clear. There could not have been any question of an unconscious suggestion on my part.

The Book of All Saints is a wonderful gift to the Church because it shows how the saints pray and because it invites us—by contagion, as it were—to pray ourselves. The apostles and many representatives of the primitive Church are among the figures portrayed. In the book *The Mission of the Prophets* (*Die Sendung der Propheten*, 1953), Adrienne also portrayed Old Testament figures in a similar way. This provides a transition to another side of her charism that will be discussed in what follows. It was intended to give fresh recognition to the colorful variety of viewpoints of the "spiritualities" not only in the communion of saints, but in Holy Scripture as well. In order to give an idea of these prayer portraits, we have selected three modern examples at random.

PIUS X (1835–1914)

I hear his prayer. It is perhaps in the most profound sense a papal prayer. He was pious when he became pope, very devoted to the welfare of the Church, with a scholarship nourished by his piety, with true simplicity of heart not opposed by his intelligence. But all that he was did not coalesce into a unity. His attitude was Christian and yet beset by weakness, his prayer sometimes lukewarm, sometimes carried by great warmth; his views were ecclesial, but he did not exert himself very much in order to defend them. He possessed a certain love for men that had not, however, recognized the commitment to the care of souls as an ultimately pressing need. When he became pope, he was terrified. He had not wanted this; not for himself, since he considered himself unworthy. Nor could he believe that they really wanted him, that the election had been conducted properly. He was afraid of an error that he had perhaps not committed but to which he had contributed. He was afraid that he had not presented himself as he really was, that he had given them a false impression of himself, that he had deceived the others somewhat; he was afraid that more importance had been attributed to his words than they actually warranted. When he realized that he had to assume the office irrevocably, he saw in this an occasion for a change, a conversion, for an integration of his task with his talents. The new task had to be unified with what God had given him to do long ago. He saw that what he was capable of becoming was far from what he personally expected and desired and respected in a pope. He saw himself as dissipated, full of faults. The papal office would have to make something out of him, something only attainable through daily effort. He was determined to take this work upon himself, first of all in the sense of a "meritorious achievement", until it suddenly became clear to him: only the presence of Christ can accomplish this. The authority of Saint Peter, as transferred to him by Christ, must rise again in Pius in the Christ-Peter confrontation: a vital, paternal authority, embracing the whole Church, one that makes him the Father of all Christendom; not so that this title of Father would be acquired once and for all, but rather so that it would arise ever fresh and alive out of the Lord's presence.

And now the Eucharist appears to him as the guarantee for this presence of the Lord, the guarantee for the general accomplishment of what he must accomplish in himself, the guarantee also for a revitalization of the papacy. From now on, his prayers revolve around Communion, his entreaties around this power of the Presence. There is much that he discards, much that he even loses with regard to outward forms and practices of his former piety, for the sake of the one task: to be present before Christ, to live in Christ through Christ's renewed work in him.

This demand becomes so intense that from now on he sees the world, the Church, his loved ones, in the light of the Eucharist; he examines everything through the power of Communion—in fact, *lets* everything be examined on this basis. He looks for the presence of the Lord everywhere. He had always felt the penetrating, absolute actuality of the eucharistic presence. But now this reality has become something so real, so active for him, so implanted in his mission, that he becomes its apostle. And he seeks to integrate everything into this idea, tries to love and let love. He understands the power of love, not in the Johannine sense of a personal, loving following of Christ, but rather in the sense of a participation, through grace, in what is most sublime. He sees it coming down from above in a living stream in which he is allowed to share; and therefore he must give his share as well. His life becomes ever more clear and transparent; he himself vanishes in order to let only what is of the Lord live. There is probably much that he had previously thought, examined, considered that now simply withers, vanishes, and becomes unimportant to him, because what is important must hold first place and because it is clear that nothing secondary must be allowed to dispute this place. And he succeeds in living in this attitude of prayer, no longer falling out of it, but living in it as the Lord desires. Here—without having consciously aspired to do so—he takes the place of a John, one who is friend and beloved. Thus he is someone who has made the love of the Lord real within himself and experiences it in a living way.

MERCIER (1851–1926)

I see his prayer; it somehow has a beautiful form but lacks content. He forms his personal prayer into a kind of liturgical act, gives it a whole system, a rhythm, a structure. He sees himself, moreover, as somehow leading the prayers of an invisible community, but he is not humble. He considers, not what he is praying, but rather *how* he is praying, in a sort of exterior attitude of submission. This is where he puts the emphasis. Nevertheless, he is animated deeply by the desire to please God. But he begins outside of himself. Therefore he cannot even find the right relationship with men, one based on humble love. He constructs, as it were, a theory of Christianity, of its efficacy and consequences; and this theory encompasses everything except himself. He perceives himself as the transmitter of an energy that, nevertheless, does not make use of him just now in order to communicate itself. The contact does not pass through him; the waves of power spread out, but they pass him by. And yet he is zealous, respects every new idea, is a good partner in conversation, wants to serve the Church and God and work for a unity of faith that would at the same time be a unity of the Church. But a Church where very much would be form and one that would necessarily lack inner ardor, because he himself would be incapable of letting it burn within him and of kindling it in others.

He has, on the human level, sound judgment of what is possible or impossible in the affairs of the Church. But his efficacy does not penetrate deeply because he does not pray deeply. And when he constructs theories, he does so mainly from ideas he has picked up someplace; ideas he has found clear and persuasive and that he can then invest with a certain power due to his widespread influence, but without an ultimate, unconditional, inner conviction on his part.

EDITH STEIN (1891–1942)

I see her groping, astonished prayer, which in the beginning seems like a conversation with herself, one that is very *controlled*. It is almost like a question that she would pose to herself in the not wholly conscious belief that she might not have to finish the incomplete sentence or fully state the question. Perhaps God might intervene in the middle of the sentence, might make his presence known and answer her question in much greater depth than she herself could or would even be capable of expecting. And God does truly answer. She prays more and more and finally receives a triumphant assurance and rejoices. From this moment of triumphant certainty on, everything is perfectly simple and straightforward. She will walk the way that God points out to her; she belongs to him; she has regained her childlike joy, a joy that has increased and become more self-evident through love, through faith. It would be completely wrong to assume that her philosophical knowledge is of any help to her in her struggle for faith. It is incidental. She has to revise certain matters to accommodate them to the faith she has gained. But she need not mix them, need not reexamine each definition and each formula in order to construct to some extent a basis for faith from philosophy.

Faith imposes upon her the very conscious obligation to make a clean sweep of her faults, to concentrate on a kind of holiness and awaken it in herself. It hovers before her as an absolute demand, not in the sense of a personal mission, but in gratitude to God who has called her. She does it in order to assume somehow the customs that are required in God's environment, in order to be educated by him in such a way that he can tolerate her presence. She prays much and readily and becomes increasingly humble and transparent. It is no sacrifice for her—not even a sacrifice of her intellect—to renounce her previous profession and to become what God demands from her.

For her, Carmel is obedience and poverty, contemplative life in anonymity, commitment to the Church where she requires commitment, and, particularly, the increase of the Church's wealth of prayer. Carmel is a place where one thinks only of God, lives only for him, where what is personal is effaced so that what is God's can become alive and radiant.

Philosophy means much less to her in the monastery than one might assume. She is pressured from outside to pursue it; she works on it under an obedience that she has not chosen herself and would not have chosen. It is true that she is independent and educated in her thinking and writing so that it is less difficult for her than other external activities. And, it is true that she would like to fulfill the task in a way that would awaken an attentiveness to religious questions among many thinkers. But it cannot be said that this is her mission. Her mission is that of *preferring* the religious life to the successes and battles and noise in the world. But external events somehow obscure this inner core of her mission. She is concerned, not with refuge in the human sense, but, rather, with a final refuge in God, with the final decision for him alone.

Martyrdom becomes the crowning of her mission, becomes her entrance into still greater anonymity, as a carrying of Christ's presence to the ultimate place of suffering. And yet it is almost as if the main emphasis of her mission rests on her entrance into Carmel even more than on her martyrdom.

The Diversity of Spiritualities in Holy Scripture

This diversity is quite obvious to the attentive reader of Adrienne's commentaries on Scripture. The exegesis of the Johannine texts is in the spirit of John; the Pauline ones, in the spirit of Paul; the letter of James and the letters of Peter, in their spirit, respectively. That means that the essential concerns of each of these four major early Christian spiritualities are considered from its special frame of reference. It is not surprising that, running through all differences, Adrienne's spirituality (which is so close to Marian spirituality) reveals itself. Nor is it surprising that her own orientation coincides on several grounds with the Johannine one: (1) it was part of the mission of the new foundation, in which Ignatian spirituality was to be traced back to its Johannine sources and origins; (2) Adrienne tended toward a certain feminine quality of the Johannine attitude, which, moreover, (3) is itself closely related to the Marian one. She related least well with Paul; there is much to read in her diary on this subject: the placing of his own personality in the forefront, the exhortation to imitate him (as he imitates Christ) was difficult to reconcile with Adrienne's spirit of "effacement". The religious significance of her commentaries will be discussed below. What is important here is the task (which for once runs parallel with today's biblical study) of differentiating the points of view. God is far too great for *one* single perspective to contain everything essential. On the other hand, God is also much too free to inspire a sacred writer in only one way. In a (somewhat fragmentary) treatise, Adrienne sought to portray the different *modes of inspiration*, for example, those of the evangelists. The diaries likewise contain an abundance of similar remarks. I know of none of Adrienne's countless visions, of which she related only a fraction, that would not have contained an evident "spiritual fruit" valid for everyone.

The Fisher's Net

This was our title for the book that offers one (*one*, not *the*!) interpretation of the Johannine number of 153 fish in

Peter's net. Of all her books, this is the one that was most truly a "gift". Only a very incomplete introduction to it can be presented here. It can and should serve as proof of how little Adrienne derived her inspiration from a worldly source. It will remain a hard nut to crack for all psychoanalysts and their like. One hundred fifty-three is here the total of the Church's holiness, an integration of the prime numbers contained therein as distinct principles of holiness that are represented by certain chosen saints. For a long time, only the first basic seven were given (from 11 to 31, since the numbers up to 10 belong to the Divinity; 5, however, is Mary), then the system was extended to 53 (= John), then to 153 (with the last prime number being 151 = Peter). Each time Adrienne knew the numbers and combinations of numbers, with which whole biographies of saints could be constructed, before she had any idea who the bearer of this number was. At times it was I who had to "guess" it, or the name was dropped quite casually during a dictation months later. To give an example, one day she dictated the following to me:

$$97 + (3 \times 17) + 5$$
$$97 + (2 \times 19) + 17 + 1$$
$$97 + (4 \times 13) + 4$$
$$97 + (2 \times 19) + 11 + 7$$
$$97 + (5 \times 11) + 1$$
$$97 + (4 \times 11) + 12$$
$$97 + (4 \times 11) + 7 + 5$$
$$97 + 31 + 12 + 5 + 7 + 1$$
$$97 + 53 + 3$$

First of all, it will be noted that every line adds up to 153. That means that the saint in question, 97, rounds off, by means of distinct principles of holiness (or even "patronages") to the holiness of the Church. Eleven is Ignatius (1–1: *Deus semper maior*, and also: the naked God before naked man); 13 is Paul (1–3, the God of the Old Covenant, leading to the Trinity); 17 is Francis of Assisi (God flowing into the charisms of the Spirit); 19 is Vianney (confession, 9 is also always the number of God's mystery); 23 is Irenaeus (as the first theologian; 2 = the God-man, interpreted with the Trinity in view); 29 is Canisius (obedience, Christ, who surrenders himself into the mystery of God); 31 is Monica (as representing the *ecclesia orans*— Augustine will be 131). Two is the God-man; 3, the Trinity; 4, the Cross; 5, Mary; 7, the Spirit. One can now show how 97 is defined in 9 different phases of his existence by the components of his spirituality.

The selection of the saints in *Das Fischernetz* (The fisher's net) naturally remains an arbitrary one from a human point of view; those saints are also, of course, largely representative of the countless number of others. And, naturally, this selection is also intentionally tailored to the spirituality to be represented in our foundations and contains saints whom we know and love and who are close to us. Also it was always stressed that the "mathematics" displayed here shows only a minute glimpse of the infinite mathematics of the heavenly Jerusalem, never reducible to any system. But what this astonishing book is really teaching us (and this cannot even be outlined here) is this: that there is an absolute *correspondence* between heaven and earth. The correspondence between Christ and the will of the Father is perfect, but so is the correspondence between the assent of Mary-Ecclesia and the demand of the Word. And there is the possibility of letting oneself be rounded out into the Church (153), of being brought to completion, through the community of saints. And furthermore: the word of God to man is precise, and the expected obedience should be just as precise, not vague and approximate. Finally, the great missions of the saints are (as prime numbers) indivisible. They originate from the unity and uniqueness of God. Examples of missions presumed to be of major importance, which at first sight look like prime numbers but then prove to be divisible after all—which means they have been invented and pieced together by man—are instructive; they lack an ultimate transparency and also fruitfulness.

Those portions of the commentary on the Book of Revelation (*Die Apokalypse*) which deal with numbers also demonstrate that the "system" of the heavenly Jerusalem corresponds to an infinite "mathematics" that cannot be captured in temporal terms. But the grand finale of this commentary, with its interpretation of the heavenly city, again demonstrates that all these numbers are only forms of infinite love, as indeed all configurations in the temporal Church are crystallized forms of God's love, invented for us sinners.

Experiential Dogmatics

A great number of Adrienne's statements about Catholic doctrine have been collected and systematized according to the articles of the Apostles' Creed (*Das Wort und die Mystik*, Teil II: *Objektive Mystik* [The word and mysticism, part 2: Objective mysticism]). Not all of the articles have been equally developed, if only for the reason that important statements (for example, about the Passion and the descent into hell) had to be placed in a different context. This great work remains a fragment, and, if it can be said that any of Adrienne's works could have been still more fully developed, then it is true of this one. Adrienne, who never remembered what she had already dictated or in which order I assembled the shorthand notes, even said in her last years of life, "How I would have liked doing a book on dogmatics!" Well, in her way she did write one, at least she provided important contributions to it.

Mysticism is defined in the textbooks as *cognitio experimentalis Dei*: an experiential awareness of the reality and nature of God. If, however, God is revealed for the Christian in salvation history, centrally in Jesus Christ and his Church, then it is actually incomprehensible that this *cognitio experimentalis* should not include, above all, the ways in which God is revealed among us; whether it be Christ himself in his existence (and his consciousness), his suffering and Resurrection, his presence in the Eucharist and the other sacraments, whether it be the Holy Spirit and his inspirations and other modes of operation in the Church. It goes without saying that the mystical experience neither replaces nor even weakens the act of faith; rather, it has faith as its basis in order to flow back into it renewed, enriched. There is, of course, no glaring contradiction between faith and vision. But there is an economy in the life of every Christian and of every saint, according to which in decisive moments he is placed in the realm of naked faith (John of the Cross!) and must do without any consolation from vision or illuminating assurance.

The main emphasis of this work as we now have it lies (1) on the impossibility of comprehending God and his self-revelation; that is, the connection between heaven and earth, (2) on the Incarnation of Christ, his human-divine consciousness (this included some actual "experiments"), (3) on his path toward suffering, (4) his trial, which is presented here primarily in the already-mentioned treatise on purgatory (as the existential dimension of Christ's trial), and (5) on the doctrine of the Holy Spirit and his effects in the Church, in Scripture, and in the sacraments.

It was, and will remain, difficult to make strict divisions here as everywhere in Adrienne's writings. Since she dictated only for a short period daily, we have, along with the continuing commentary, an immense number of individual statements that could be inserted elsewhere just as well as here. The reader of her works must constantly remember that what cannot be found in one place may surface someplace else. A systematic index to her whole work will prove indispensable one day. The diaries also contain a great deal that is of dogmatic significance. However, I have retained in them mainly those sections which relate more personal matters, while putting in *Objektive Mystik* instead those sections which—more removed from the person—are of a more objective character.

Theory of Mysticism

As has already become apparent from the preceding range of topics, Adrienne's *theory of mysticism*—again compiled from numerous individual statements (*Das Wort und die Mystik*, Teil I: *Subjektive Mystik* [The word and mysticism, part 1: Subjective mysticism])—is of a revolutionary character in the tradition of the Church. She breaks radically with the pointed Protestant Either/Or that Emil Brunner advanced in his book *Mysticism and the Word*: either mysticism (where religious experience then becomes the ultimate criterion: Schleiermacher!) or the Word, with pure faith as its correlative. Adrienne, on the other hand, has in mind from the outset a faith experience that corresponds to the biblical experience of faith in the Old and New Covenant. Thus, a first part deals with the biblical "mysticism" of the prophets, Jesus himself, and his disciples. Furthermore (as already mentioned), the usual abrupt opposition between habitual grace (unfolded in the "gifts of the Holy Spirit") and charisms (which in some circumstances can be possessed and exercised even without the possession of grace, as would be customarily illustrated with such questionable examples as Balaam) is overcome: authentic charism as a service of a member of the Church to the community can normally only be exercised in grace. A second part treats distinct individual charisms, which, on the one hand, are well known in the Church and, on the other hand, correspond to certain experiences peculiar to Adrienne; a third part, possibly the most important, deals with the criteria of authentic mysticism, which are, essentially, the quality of the assent, the sheer readiness to serve, the willingness to transmit, the personal anonymity, the total transparency to the Word of God. The "tests of readiness" for individual saints—especially women mystics—as included in the second part of the *Book of All Saints*, form the concrete illustrative material for this theory. Together they explain why at times certain so-called "private revelations"—which were, nonetheless, not unimportant and contained a message for the entire Church—either did not "succeed" or gained acceptance in a not entirely credible way and eventually had to be first purified and completed by theologians or the Magisterium itself. The transmitting medium had just not been pure, not selfless enough; the vision or insight had been clouded through the self-reflection of the visionary so that he (or she) had been paying more attention to matters of secondary importance while the crucial matter had been slighted.

Adrienne von Speyr has brought mysticism back from the clandestine existence into which, increasingly misunderstood, indeed scorned, it had been exiled and silenced by official theology and proclamation and has returned it to the center of salvation history. This center is the exchange between the Word of God in Christ and the hearing and responding to this Word by the Bride-Church. Within the context of the commentaries on Scripture, the question has to be raised: Who is the adequate subject for hearing the Word? Who will hear it in the way it is said and intended, in the way it seeks to be understood and believed? Is it the people who only hear the Ten Commandments and have then had enough and leave any further listening to Moses (Deut 5:23–26)—or is it Moses, who stands his ground before the consuming fire and listens to the end, so as, much later, to proclaim and then interpret to the people what he has received, including the great commandment he has heard? What deserves to be called mysticism—not in the vague sense of the history and philosophy of religion, but rather in the Catholic-ecclesial sense—occurs when God's Word is heard, not only with exegetical and theological understanding, but with the whole heart, the whole being, when one is steadfast before the self-disclosure of the heart of God despite fire and night.

One of the most astonishing charismatic phenomena in Adrienne's life confirms what has just been said. And even if it seems hardly credible to some, I must nevertheless attest to it exactly as I witnessed it in the year 1945. I record here an unrevised page from my diary of that time.

The Apocalypse

We were in Estavayer at Neuenburg Lake. I was giving the spiritual exercises that were intended as the founding act for our community.

"On the evening of August 9th, after Adrienne had been experiencing anxiety for a long time, she said to me before a conference, 'Come straight to my room afterward.' I found her greatly confused. She kept repeating, 'I cannot hold her any longer, I cannot hold her any longer ...!' I asked her to tell me all that had happened.... She did so, as well as she could, and it even went quite well. Once in a while she would stop and ask, 'Does this still make any sense? Say so, if you think I am crazy.' She told me that a terrible thunderstorm had suddenly begun. There had been lightning, thunder, then a massive earthquake. Hail had then followed. She had stepped out on the veranda to find out what was going on, but she did not get wet. That is when she realized that this thunderstorm was not an external, natural one. She was caught in a strange tension for she saw simultaneously the earthly evening sky, which was quite calm, and the other, totally agitated landscape that she was experiencing interiorly. Then she suddenly saw heaven opened (in the following I am keeping strictly to the words she used), and she saw a woman in the opening. She was so radiant that Adrienne, whose eyes had recently become weaker anyway, was blinded (even afterward she still complained that she was hardly able to see anymore because of the sheer brightness). The woman had twelve stars around her head; Adrienne had counted them. She said: 'I am almost entirely certain that there are twelve. She is entirely wrapped in fire and stands on a globe. She was pregnant and was crying out during the entire time. Don't you hear how she is crying out? Do you really not hear?'

"I asked her, 'On what kind of globe is she standing?'

"Adrienne was as if in a trance; she got up, took off one shoe, and tested the ground with her foot. 'It is the moon', she said; 'Yes, it is most certainly the moon.'

"Then she saw a dragon appear; it was red and had seven heads, ten horns, and seven diadems on its heads. I asked her what was happening with the dragon.

" 'I don't know!' she said. 'He is simply enraged, and he is very powerful. He is evil, the devil.' Then she looked around, 'What are those blood basins doing over there?... And do tell me, what does John have to do with all of this? He is present somehow, but he is not visible in the picture.' Suddenly she looked at me, deathly afraid, 'Who is this woman? Is she ... the Mother?' Adrienne came and held out her hands to me, 'I promise you obedience, absolute obedience; I want only to be an instrument for God. But this Woman must be helped; she must be supported.' She then began to explain to me how women are assisted during the first stage of labor. 'You have to support them by pressing their backs firmly with your hand to give strength, or rather the feeling of strength. And you must take hold of their shoulders at the same time.' She told me that she had often done this for long periods of time in the delivery room and how extremely exhausting it was. And she would have to do the same now for the woman, and she herself had no more strength left. What should be done? Everything was so difficult because the image was so fragmented. I asked her why. She said, 'Everything is so disjointed, so incoherent—the thunderstorm, the hail, the woman, the bright light, the red beast ... it is so tiring; it tears one apart. Do you really not hear her crying out?'

"I then opened the New Testament and read Revelation 11:19 to 12:3 to her. She was totally motionless.

" 'What is that?'

"I said, 'John.'

" 'But we have certainly not read this in the Gospels?'

" 'No, it is the Apocalypse.'

" 'My God, the Apocalypse!' After some time she continued: 'I have never read it. I had begun once, years ago, but I did not get beyond the first chapter. It was simply too vast, too incomprehensible for me ... But then who is that woman?'

"I said, 'Mary and the Church in one.'

"She said, 'You are right. That is true. Now I understand ... Mary is crying out because she foresees the fate of her Son. She does not cry out because of her own pains; she cries out in anticipation, in the distinct awareness of her Son's pains. While she is in labor, she suffers in advance a portion of her Son's suffering. And the Church cries out but without this foreknowledge. She cries out for the unforeseeable suffering of her children, simply for their destiny in general, but even she cries in anticipation. This they have in common. What can be done?'

"I said, 'Help ...'"

This was the beginning of that unique, truly apocalyptic dictation (all the others occurred in perfect calmness), one with transports, digressions. Adrienne saw the images directly before her eyes, and each time she was able to recite the corresponding text without having read it; I wrote down and preserved those texts she recited. She dictated chapters 12 to 19 or 20, followed by chapters 1–11, and then the conclusion, chapters 20–22. In connection with the first verse, she developed a whole theory of a specifically apocalyptic vision and a state of total objectivity in which the visionary is distant both from earth and heaven. Just as the dictation of the middle and the beginning had been wild and dramatic, so that of the end was wonderfully radiant. In connection with chapters 21 and 22, she heard "prayers of heaven" that were not included in the commentary and that can be read in this book at the end of the "Prayers".

What the exegetes might say about all this does not concern me here; I can answer for one thing: what Adrienne, without knowing the scriptural text, had seen portrayed in the most minute detail and had then interpreted was not subjective imagination. The explanations that she herself gives can be read in the commentary as well as in her theory of mysticism. She speaks of an objective world of images that belongs to divine revelation and is granted by God in different, analogous ways; Daniel certainly participated in this: see her "Interpretation of Daniel" in the appendix of the book on *Isaias* (1958).

Bodily Manifestations

I have mentioned that Adrienne had a wound under her breast dating from the first Marian vision in 1917. She perceived this as a mysterious seal, a reminder, and a promise. After her conversion, this wound was sharply accentuated, and other stigmata were at times manifested along with it. Even if much of these bodily manifestations of Adrienne was at the time and will forever remain mysterious, it is certain that she was chosen not only to understand spiritually the truths of Christian revelation, or to live them in a spiritual-mystical way, but also to experience them in her total existence, even bodily. The uninterrupted series of pains imposed on her, her voluntary penitential exercises, assumed under obedience, played a very decisive part in this. As already mentioned, they proved to be astonishingly fruitful. Similarly, she was charged with considering in a Christian way, from the sphere of pure *agape*, through this incarnational process, the sphere of *eros*. This corresponds to the fundamental Pauline principle that interprets the man-woman relation (without sublimations, in their authentic, created sexuality) in the light of the relation between Christ and the Church. In all sexual matters, she had a natural simplicity similar to that of Saint Hildegard, whom she greatly revered. Both of them were physicians and knew no prudery but, on the other hand, no obscure lust, either. Adrienne devoted a number of notes to the explication of *eros* in the light of *agape*; these have been gathered into a book, *Theologie der Geschlechter* (Theology of the sexes), and her numerous scattered notes about medical ethics would (at least in part) merit publication as well. As foundress of a community following the evangelical counsels, Adrienne praised virginity in many places in her works; of course she always saw it (in a Marian way) in a functional relationship to obedience. But she equally understood the sexual relationship between man and woman—and, in fact, precisely in the highest possible opposition of their functions and attitudes, with no leveling of differences—which she described in the Pauline sense as a *magnum mysterium*: "I mean in reference to Christ and the Church" (Eph 5:32).

With this we have closed our circle of Adrienne's most important individual charisms; it can only be considered a complete circle, however, when the interrelationship of all these separate themes has become evident. Whoever looks at the work as a whole from the inside will find that each theme is directly related to every other theme. What has been pointed out does not exhaust the subject. A number of things had to remain in shadow, for example the theme of the Eucharist, which plays a very important role in the background. But enough for now.

Charisms are not distributed at random but are dispensed by God to supply what is needful and lacking in his Church at each historical moment. If they are from God, they usually do not flow with the latest fashionable trend but much more likely contain an antidote and remedy for the perils of the time. In Adrienne's case, this happened quite automatically; it had indeed been prepared well in advance, long before the specific poisons that she was to counteract broke out with virulence. She cannot, therefore, be classified as a reactionary phenomenon; the great light that radiates from her existence and her work needs no shadow in order to be seen.

III

THE WORK

THE FORM OF HER WORK

Many a reader who has followed this enumeration of extraordinary charisms will be disturbed. He will with good reason suspend his judgment about the authenticity of such phenomena, at least until the Church has made a pronouncement. One can only encourage him to do so and, until then, to refrain from all hasty conclusions one way or the other. But he should be made aware of one thing that seems fundamental: surveying the form of Adrienne von Speyr's works as a whole, one will find that biblical commentaries occupy the most prominent place. Almost all of these commentaries have already been published with the ecclesiastical *imprimatur* and possess their own objective validity, without it having been necessary to raise the question of to what extent they are of charismatic origin. But one thing will be obvious to any fairly well-read, unbiased reader of Christian literature: these works originate in deep, continuous, contemplative prayer. It is precisely the personal element that the author exhibits in her work and that clearly reveals the stamp of her character, her way of thinking and expressing herself, or even of translating her inspiration—if such can be presupposed—into human words, which clearly proves that the birth of these commentaries could only have taken place in the atmosphere of contemplative prayer. Can such an atmosphere be feigned for decades on end? Many spiritual persons in the Church, without further knowledge of the circumstances, have recognized at once in Adrienne von Speyr a woman of great prayer, an unselfishly loving Christian. Those commentaries on Scripture which are already in print consequently form the broad basis, accessible to all, upon which alone those more abruptly charismatic works can validly be judged and about which a well-founded judgment can already be formed.

What is essential regarding the genesis of the dictated works has already been said. Almost invariably she dictated for twenty minutes or half an hour each afternoon. Adrienne would be seated in an armchair with her small French Segond New Testament. She would read the verse, close her eyes, reflect for a few seconds, and then begin to dictate continuously, usually very quickly, so that, being a poor stenographer, I followed only with difficulty and frequently had to ask her to pause for a moment. The very first dictations (on the Prologue of Saint John's Gospel) were still awkward in expression. Adrienne would express thoughts and viewpoints one after the other, which then had to be connected coherently to one another in a final redaction. But soon she was so accustomed to dictating that she spoke fluently, and in the last years what she dictated was often ready for direct publication. I later made a fair copy of all that had been dictated, making insignificant stylistic changes. I left out filler words, for example, like "actually" or "somehow" or "so to say", which she had used in order to gain time to formulate her thoughts, but nothing of her thought was ever changed. In order to insure the possibility of verifying this, I have kept several hundred pages of the original dictation and will make

them available when desired so they can be compared with
my final copy.

Though it is impossible to draw a distinct dividing line
between "ordinary" and "purely mystical" works, I intentionally refrained from publishing the more obviously
charismatic works during the author's lifetime—it would
have unnecessarily upset her life and that of her family.
Rather, I classified them under the collective title *Nachlasswerke* (Posthumous works), of which there are twelve volumes. The title is not entirely accurate insofar as a few
other manuscripts, whose form is similar to those already
published, were also published posthumously.

The *Nachlasswerke* were in part planned by the author
as a unit (at least thematically)—so it was obvious that
certain statements belonged in the book about numbers,
others in the book about love and sexuality, and so on,
even if these statements were separated by long periods
of time—and in part compiled by me from separate statements. Thus the *Auftragshöllen* (Missions of hell) in volume 4 of the *Nachlasswerke* have no consistently thematic
connection with each other. This is even more true of
the diaries.

Several smaller works and even some larger ones (*Confession, The Christian State of Life*) have eleven chapters: in
Das Fischernetz, eleven is the number of Saint Ignatius.
When Adrienne began such a book, she would ordinarily
dictate the headings of the eleven chapters very rapidly and
without forethought. Later I occasionally had to remind
her of the heading for the following chapter.

Regarding the form of all the dictated books—the commentaries on Scripture as well as the others—it is essential
to keep in mind that dictation occurred only for a brief
time daily, so that, actually, a new beginning took place
each time, and each dictation had a certain inner unity. If

one wanted to use a lofty comparison, one might say that parts of her work resemble a collection of Gospel logia. Sometimes, therefore—not always, of course!—the order of the sections does not matter very much. Moreover, the person who becomes familiar with Adrienne's Scripture meditations will learn that he will go away richer if he reads only a little and meditates on it, in accord with Adrienne's own meditation, rather than if he tries to work his way rapidly through a book.

Finally, one word about the relation of these Scripture commentaries to scientific exegesis. Adrienne never, even from a distance, looked into an exegetical work. She would take a text that was deemed reliable and become all ears, as it were, in order to listen to what would be revealed to her from this text. Once again it would be good to recall what has been said about the *anima ecclesiastica*. The exegete listens as an individual to what a particular, individual text means in the historic milieu of its time and takes careful note of whatever shifts and changes it may have undergone in the course of redaction. This is an important and fruitful work that, in its domain, cannot be replaced by anything else. Adrienne, however, listened to the Word in the center of the Church's heart, where the self-revealing triune God communicates his eternal mystery of love to the beloved Bride of the Son, the Church. Every single sentence, which seen from without has a finite meaning, to be precisely differentiated from other sentences, partakes, through this interior event, of an infinity always inherent in divine Truth. Without ceasing to have a *definite* meaning, every sentence shares as the Word of God in the divine quality of the ever-more, ever-greater, and consequently ever-inexhaustible. Fundamentally, Adrienne heard all words of the New Testament as an expression of the trinitarian life. In the contemplative hearing of the Word, she experienced something of the divine quality dwelling in every word of God, which for the Christian, however, is not simply transcendental silence as non-Christian mystics might experience it, but, indeed, the ineffable Eternal Love that shines through the Incarnate Word spoken by the Father. It is by no means the case that the non-Christian mystic—freed from all the limits imposed by the world—can soar into the absolute, while the Christian mystic must always run up against and remain impeded by the rigid barriers of historic revelation and ecclesiastical dogma. Much rather is it so that the true fullness of eternal life is God's triune love-exchange, beyond which a greater conception of God is not possible. The finite forms of the revelation of this love merely open "gates of eternal life", in the words of Adrienne, who was used to going in and out through all these gates with the natural ease of a child of God who feels at home, while her words themselves reverberate with the rhythm of the waves of the eternal, divine sea.

The following is a comprehensive list of all Adrienne's writings of any importance. First listed are those writings which exist in manuscript form, followed by the series of dictated books.

WORKS IN MANUSCRIPT FORM

1. Translation of *Histoire d'une âme*, by Thérèse de Lisieux. This translation was revised by me and published by Johannesverlag: *Theresia vom Kinde Jesus: Geschichte einer Seele. In neuer Übertragung von Adrienne von Speyr. Geleitwort von Hans Urs von Balthasar* (1947). This first edition has been superseded by the critical edition that was prepared by P. François de S. Marie in 1956, translated by

Dr. O. Iserland and Cornelia Capol and published by Johannesverlag in 1958.

2. An autobiography, *Aus meinem Leben*, on 284 large sheets. It breaks off with the year 1926. It has been in print since 1968. See above, p. 19. Translated by Mary Emily Hamilton and Dennis D. Martin in *My Early Years* (San Francisco: Ignatius Press, 1995).

3. *Christiane: Briefe über Liebe und Ehe* (Christiane: Letters about love and marriage). Lucerne: Verlag J. Stocker, 1947. Only part of the manuscript has been preserved. See above, p. 53.

4. Numerous notes for a book on medical ethics, *Arzt und Patient* (Physician and patient). Einsiedeln: Johannes verlag, 1983. See above, p. 89.

5. A wealth of *Aphorisms* about the Christian life, above all about the life of the evangelical counsels. Mostly published in *Lumina* (Einsiedeln: Johannesverlag, 1969) and *Lumina und neue Lumina* (Johannesverlag, 1974). Translated by Adrian Walker as *Lumina and New Lumina* (San Francisco: Ignatius Press, 2008).

6. Many outlines for the future *Rules* of the community she founded and for the way of life and attitude of its members in general.

7. Detailed *Notes* in preparation for the dictation of her book on Mary; it was the first time that Adrienne dictated on a theme without following a text verse by verse.

8. In the beginning, when I used to edit the dictated text more heavily, Adrienne would carefully supervise the final form of a text before and during the typesetting. Many notes are preserved in which she made improvements and asked for clarifications when to her mind the thought had not been formulated with sufficient precision, and so on.

9. In the diaries of her youth, Adrienne repeatedly tried her hand at short stories and novellas. A small fragment of such a diary has been preserved. She later dictated several short stories, among them a description of her beloved grandmother's house. It is included in the autobiography listed above.

10. An abundance of letters. During the time immediately following her conversion, she used to make a kind of report on her spiritual life while I was away. In her final years, she wrote many spiritual letters; a lively correspondence with a German woman religious contains many of Adrienne's views about life in secular institutes today.

DICTATED WORKS

Commentaries on Scripture

11. *Die Schöpfung* (Creation). Einsiedeln: Johannesverlag, 1972.

12. *Elija.* Einsiedeln: Johannesverlag, 1972. Translated by Brian McNeil as *Elijah* (San Francisco: Ignatius Press, 1990).

13. *Job.* Einsiedeln: Johannesverlag, 1972.

14. *Das Hohelied* (The Song of Songs). Einsiedeln: Johannesverlag, 1972.

15. *Über Gebete im Alten Testament* (Prayer in the Old Testament). Unpublished.

16. *Isaias* (*Isaiah*). Commentary on selected texts. With an appendix on the visions in Daniel. Einsiedeln: Johannesverlag, 1958.

17. *Aus den Visionen Daniels.* Published as an appendix to *Isaias.*

18. *Achtzehn Psalmen* (Eighteen psalms). Einsiedeln: Johannesverlag, 1957.

19. *Die Sendung der Propheten*. Einsiedeln: Johannesverlag, 1953. Translated by Dr. David Kipp as *The Mission of the Prophets* (San Francisco: Ignatius Press, 1996).

20. *Die Bergpredigt* (The Sermon on the Mount). Meditations on Matthew 5–7. Einsiedeln: Johannesverlag, 1948.

21. *Passion nach Matthäus* (The Passion according to Matthew). Also includes the Resurrection account. Einsiedeln: Johannesverlag, 1957.

22. *Markus*. Adrienne von Speyr explained the Gospel of Mark in her community in the form of points for meditation. Einsiedeln: Johannesverlag, 1971. Translated by Michelle K. Borras as *Mark: Meditations for a Community* (San Francisco: Ignatius Press, 2012).

23. *Lukas* (Luke). A few separate texts as points for meditation in the community. Unpublished. Includes also some parables; see no. 23.

24. *Gleichnisse des Herrn* (Parables of the Lord). Einsiedeln: Johannesverlag, 1966.

25. *Das Johannesevangelium* (The Gospel of John) in 4 volumes. Volume 1: *Das Wort wird Fleisch: Betrachtungen über Johannes 1–5*. Einsiedeln: Johannesverlag, 1949. Translated by Sister Lucia Wiedenhöver, O.C.D., and Alexander Dru as *The Word Becomes Flesh: Meditations on John 1–5* (San Francisco: Ignatius Press, 1994).

26. Volume 2: *Die Streitreden: Betrachtungen über Johannes 6–12*. Einsiedeln: Johannesverlag, 1949. Translated by Brian McNeil, C.R.V., as *The Discourses of Controversy: Meditations on John 6–12* (San Francisco: Ignatius Press, 1993).

27. Volume 3: *Die Abschiedsreden: Betrachtungen über Johannes 13–17*. Einsiedeln: Johannesverlag, 1948. Translated by E. A. Nelson as *The Farewell Discourses: Meditations on John 13–17* (San Francisco: Ignatius Press, 1987).

28. Volume 4: *Geburt der Kirche: Betrachtungen über Johannes 18–21*. Einsiedeln: Johannesverlag, 1949. Translated by David Kipp as *The Birth of the Church: Meditations on John 18–21* (San Francisco: Ignatius Press, 1991).

29. *Apostelgeschichte* (Acts of the Apostles). Points for meditation for the whole book given to the community. Unpublished.

30. *Der Sieg der Liebe*. Einsiedeln: Johannesverlag, 1953. Translated by Sister Lucia Wiedenhöver, O.C.D., as *The Victory of Love: A Meditation on Romans 8* (San Francisco: Ignatius Press, 1990).

31. *Der erste Korintherbrief* (The First Letter to the Corinthians). Einsiedeln: Johannesverlag, 1956.

32. *Kinder des Lichtes* (Children of light). Meditations on the Letter to the Ephesians. Einsiedeln: Johannesverlag, 1950.

33. *Dienst der Freude* (Service of joy). Einsiedeln: Johannesverlag, 1951.

34. *Der Kolosserbrief.* Einsiedeln: Johannesverlag, 1957. Translated by Michael J. Miller as *The Letter to the Colossians* (San Francisco: Ignatius Press, 1998).

35. *Die katholischen Briefe* (The Catholic Letters) in 2 volumes. Volume 1: *Der Jakobusbrief. Die Petrusbriefe* (The Letter of James. The Letters of Peter). Einsiedeln: Johannesverlag, 1961.

36. Volume 2: *Die Johannesbriefe* (The Letters of John). Einsiedeln: Johannesverlag, 1961.

37. *Der Judasbrief* (The Letter of Jude). Points for meditation in the community. Unpublished.

38. *Die Apokalypse, I* (The Apocalypse, vol. 1), chapters 1–12. Einsiedeln: Johannesverlag; Vienna: Heroldverlag, 1950.

39. *Die Apokalypse, II* (The Apocalypse, vol. 2), chapters 13–22. Einsiedeln: Johannesverlag; Vienna: Heroldverlag, 1950. There is a second edition combining both volumes: Einsiedeln: Johannesverlag, 1976.

Other Writings

40. *Magd des Herrn.* Einsiedeln: Johannesverlag, 1948; 2nd ed., 1969. Translated by E. A. Nelson as *Handmaid of the Lord* (San Francisco: Ignatius Press, 1985; 2nd ed., 2017).

41. *Die Welt des Gebetes.* Einsiedeln: Johannesverlag, 1951. Translated by Graham Harrison as *The World of Prayer* (San Francisco: Ignatius Press, 1985).

42. *Die Pforten des ewigen Lebens.* Einsiedeln: Johannesverlag, 1953. Translated by Corona Sharp as *The Gates of Eternal Life* (San Francisco: Ignatius Press, 1983).

43. *Das Geheimnis des Todes.* Einsiedeln: Johannesverlag, 1953. Translated by Graham Harrison as *The Mystery of Death* (San Francisco: Ignatius Press, 1988).

44. *Das Angesicht des Vaters.* Einsiedeln: Johannesverlag, 1955. Translated by Dr. David Kipp as *The Countenance of the Father* (San Francisco: Ignatius Press, 1997).

45. *Der grenzenlose Gott.* Einsiedeln: Johannesverlag, 1955. Translated by Helena M. Tomko as *The Boundless God* (San Francisco: Ignatius Press, 2004).

46. *Sie folgten seinem Ruf: Berufung und Askese.* Einsiedeln: Johannesverlag, 1955. Translated by Erasma Leiva-Merikakis as *They Followed His Call: Vocation and Asceticism* (San Francisco: Ignatius Press, 1986).

47. *Das Licht und die Bilder: Elemente der Kontemplation.* Adoratio. Einsiedeln: Johannesverlag, 1955. Translated by David Schindler, Jr., as *Light and Images: Elements of Contemplation* (San Francisco: Ignatius Press, 2004).

48. *Christlicher Stand.* Einsiedeln: Johannesverlag, 1956. Translated by Mary Frances McCarthy as *The Christian State of Life* (San Francisco: Ignatius Press, 1986).

49. *Kreuzeswort und Sakrament.* Einsiedeln: Johannesverlag, 1957. Translated by Graham Harrison as *The Cross, Word and Sacrament* (San Francisco: Ignatius Press, 1983).

50. *Die Beichte.* Einsiedeln: Johannesverlag, 1960. Translated by Douglas W. Stott as *Confession* (San Francisco: Ignatius Press, 1985; 2nd ed., 2017).

51. *Gebetserfahrung* (The experience of prayer). Not dictated as a treatise but compiled from separate texts. Einsiedeln: Johannesverlag, 1965.

52. *Das Buch vom Gehorsam* (The book of obedience). Einsiedeln: Johannesverlag, 1966.

53. *Der Mensch vor Gott.* Einsiedeln: Johannesverlag, 1966. Translated by Nicholas J. Healy and D. C. Schindler as *Man before God* (San Francisco: Ignatius Press, 2009).

54. *Aussagen über sich selbst.* Published in this present volume. Einsiedeln: Johannesverlag, 1968. Translated by Antje Lawry and Sister Sergia Englund, O.C.D., as "Statements of Adrienne von Speyr about Herself", in *First Glance at Adrienne von Speyr* (San Francisco: Ignatius Press, 1980; 2nd ed., 2017).

55. *Gebete*. Published in this volume. Einsiedeln: Johannesverlag, 1968. Translated by Antje Lawry and Sister Sergia Englund, O.C.D., as "Prayers", in *First Glance at Adrienne von Speyr* (San Francisco: Ignatius Press, 1980; 2nd ed., 2017).

56. *Drei Frauen und der Herr*. Magdalen and faith, the penitent woman of Luke 7 and hope, Mary of Bethany and love. Einsiedeln: Johannesverlag, 1978. Translated by Graham Harrison as *Three Women and the Lord* (San Francisco: Ignatius Press, 1986).

57. *Passion von innen*. Separate meditations in connection with Saint Matthew's Passion. Einsiedeln: Johannesverlag, 1981. Translated by Sister Lucia Wiedenhöver, O.C.D., as *Passion from Within* (San Francisco: Ignatius Press, 1998).

58. *Die heilige Messe*. Einsiedeln: Johannesverlag, 1980. Translated by Helena M. Saward as *The Holy Mass* (San Francisco: Ignatius Press, 1999).

59. *Über die Liebe* (On Love). The last treatise dictated in complete form: 1955/1956. Einsiedeln: Johannesverlag, 1976.

60. *Fragmente* (Fragments). Fragments of three treatises that had been completely planned and begun: "On Courage"; "On Asceticism"; "On Salvation". Unpublished.

61. *Das Kirchenjahr* (*The Church Year*). Not dictated as a treatise but compiled from numerous separate meditations about Christian feasts. Unpublished.

62. *Bereitschaft: Dimensionen christlichen Gehorsams* (Readiness: Dimensions of Christian obedience). Einsiedeln: Johannesverlag, 1975.

63. *Bei Gott und bei den Menschen: Gebete.* Ginsiedeln: Johannesverlag, 1992. Translated by Adrian Walker as *With God and with Men* (San Francisco: Ignatius Press, 1995).

64. *Das Themenheft* (The notebook). Einsiedeln: Johannesverlag, 1977.

65. *Maria in der Erlösung.* Einsiedeln: Johannesverlag, 1979. Translated by Helena M. Tomko as *Mary in the Redemption* (San Francisco: Ignatius Press, 2003).

The Twelve "Posthumous Works"

66. Volume 1 in two half-volumes: *Das Allerheiligenbuch.* Einsiedeln: Johannesverlag, 1966. See above, pp. 69ff. Translated by D. C. Schindler as *The Book of All Saints*, pt. 1 (San Francisco: Ignatius Press, 2008).

67. Volume 2: *Das Fischernetz* (The Fisher's Net). Interpretation of the number 153 as a function of the prime numbers of the saints. Einsiedeln: Johannesverlag, 1969. See above, pp. 77ff.

68. Volume 3: *Kreuz und Hölle I: Die Passionen* (Cross and hell, I: The Passions). Contains the accounts of all Passions and Holy Saturdays from 1941 to 1965. Einsiedeln: Johannesverlag, 1966. See above, pp. 35, 63ff.

69. Volume 4: *Kreuz und Hölle II: Die Auftragshöllen* (Cross and Hell, II: The missions of hell). Einsiedeln: Johannesverlag, 1972. See above, pp. 64f.

70. Volume 5: *Das Wort und die Mystik, Teil I: Subjektive Mystik* (The word and mysticism, pt. 1: Subjective mysticism). The theory of mystical experience as part of biblical revelation; the kinds and criteria of authentic mysticism. Einsiedeln: Johannesverlag, 1970. See above, pp. 82ff.

71. Volume 6: *Das Wort und die Mystik, Teil II: Objektive Mystik* (The word and mysticism, pt. 2: Objective mysticism). "Experiential dogmatics" in the form of an interpretation of the articles of faith. Einsiedeln: Johannesverlag, 1970. See above, pp. 8off.

72. Volume 7: *Das Geheimnis der Jugend* (The mystery of youth). An autobiography in the form of a return (under obedience) to the consciousness of the child, the adolescent girl, continuing up to the year of her conversion, 1940. What the handwritten autobiography describes from the recollection of the mature woman, this book describes in the immediacy of each event. Since much of this took place in conversations between Adrienne and myself, her subsequent confessor thus becomes here a mysterious companion of her Protestant years. Einsiedeln: Johannesverlag, 1966. See above, pp. 19ff.

73–75. Volumes 8–10: *Tagebücher* (Diaries). This extensive collection of documents begins with my own descriptions of Adrienne's life, experiences, and sayings even prior to the time of the dictations and gradually gives place to the numerous accounts that I took down in shorthand and arranged chronologically within the corpus of the diaries. Einsiedeln: Johannesverlag, 1975 and 1976.

76. Volume 11: *Ignatius von Loyola* (Ignatius of Loyola). A book rich in content that begins with a commentary on the autobiography of Saint Ignatius and on parts of his diaries. It includes various statements about him and also a treatise about the specifically Ignatian doctrine of Christian obedience.

Einsiedeln: Johannesverlag, 1974. The treatise on Ignatian obedience has since been published separately as *Bereitschaft: Dimension Christlichen Gehorsams* (Readiness: Dimensions of Christian obedience). Einsiedeln: Johannesverlag, 1975.

77. Volume 12: *Theologie der Geschlechter* (Theology of the sexes). Einsiedeln: Johannesverlag, 1969. See above, p. 57.

PUBLISHED ARTICLES

78. "Bemerkungen zu Paul Tournier: De la Solitude à la Communauté" (Observations on Paul Tournier's "From Solitude to Community"). *Schweizerische Rundschau*, vol. 44 (July 1944).

79. "Vom Sinn der Krankheit" (The meaning of sickness). *Festschrift für Albert Oeri*. Basel, 1945.

80. "Das Adventslicht" (Light of Advent). *Die Schweizerin*, vol. 36, no. 2 (November 1948).

81. "Heiligkeit im Alltag" (Holiness in daily life). *Geist und Leben*, vol. 22, no. 3 (June 1949).

82. "Vom lesenden Arzt" (The reading physician). *Festschrift für Fritz Ernst*. Zurich, 1949.

83. "Eine alarmierende Erscheinung: Die Gefährdung des klösterlichen Nachwuchses" (An alarming phenomenon: The endangering of new monastic vocations). *Die Schweizerin*, vol. 37, no. 3 (January 1950).

84. "Priesterliches Leben aus dem Gebet" (Priestly life sustained by prayer). *Gloria Dei*, vol. 4, no. 4 (1949/1950).

85. "Maria und die Propheten" (Mary and the prophets). *Der Christliche Sonntag*, August 13, 1950, Freiburg im Breisgau.

86. "Kirche als Mysterium". *Schweizerische Rundschau* 11/ 12 (1953).

87. "Auferstehung in uns" (Resurrection in us). *Der Christliche Weg: Kulturbeilage der kath. Solothurner Press*, vol. 2 no. 7 (1956).

ANTHOLOGIES

88. Barbara Albrecht. *Eine Theologie des Katholischen: Enführung in das Werk Adriennes von Speyr* (A theology of the Catholic: Introduction to the work of Adrienne von Speyr). Vol. 1: *Durchblick in Texten* (An overview of the texts). Einsiedeln: Johannesverlag, 1972.

89. Hans Urs von Balthasar. *Kostet und seht: Ein theologisches Lesebuch* (Come and see: A theological reader). Einsiedeln: Johannesverlag, 1988.

PART II

STATEMENTS OF
ADRIENNE VON SPEYR
ABOUT HERSELF

1. THE MOTHER OF GOD VISION[1]

In this same month of November 1917, I awoke very early one morning—it was barely even light—because of a golden light that filled the whole wall above my bed. And I saw the Mother of God as in a picture, surrounded by various people (these were standing somewhat farther back, while she was right in the foreground) as well as by several angels, some of which were as big as she was, others as small as children. The whole thing was like a picture; yet the Mother of God was alive, in heaven, and the angels were changing their positions. I think this lasted for a long time; I gazed as in a wordless prayer and was overwhelmed with admiration: never had I seen anything so beautiful. In the beginning, all of the light was like brilliantly sparkling gold, then it slowly faded, and while it faded the features of the Virgin Mary became more prominent. I was not frightened in any way, but rather filled by a new, strong, and very tender joy. Not for a moment did the whole thing strike me as unreal; it did not occur to me that I could be the victim of an illusion.

If I remember correctly, I did not tell anybody about it except Madeleine, to whom I reported the event as something quite natural. Mad simply replied, "I would have liked to have seen her, too." We never talked about it again. The memory of this vision remained intensely alive for me. For a long time it accompanied me like a wonderful secret. I now possessed, as it were, a place of refuge. Later I would have liked to have spoken about it to someone. Once or twice I felt tempted to go to see a priest and

[1] In longhand. From the autobiography (above, no. 2).

to talk to him about it, but of course I did not know any. It would never have occurred to me to talk to a Protestant pastor about it, although I do not believe that at that time I in any way knew that I had to become Catholic. From the time of the vision on, I retained from afar a tenderness for the Mother of God. I knew that one had to love her, but this did not give rise to a deeper uneasiness in me. As soon as I seriously began my instructions in the Catholic faith, however, I spoke about it to the priest who was instructing me; it was obvious to me that I had to do this.

When the Mother of God vanished, I knelt down beside my bed (I had made this a habit since my birthday), and I think I remained in prayer until it was time to go to school.

2. ENCOUNTER WITH IGNATIUS[2]

At home we always celebrated Christmas on the 24th. This year—it was in 1908—Hélène had a party in the small private school that she attended at the time under the two Loze sisters, who to us seemed infinitely old and who were probably between thirty and forty years old then. Aunt Jeanne had come from the Waldau to spend the day with us. She came very seldom; apart from Christmas in 1917, this was the only time that she came to La Chaux-de-Fonds in winter. Aunt Jeanne and I were to pick up Hélène after her school celebration; Maman admonished me strictly, "You understand me!"—under no circumstance was I to accept anything to eat from the two Loze sisters. They were too poor for it to be permissible to accept any of their delicacies. Yet at the same time they were so gracious that they would undoubtedly

[2] In longhand, as a postscript to the autobiography (see above, no. 2).

offer me some; I was to remain firm and say no. Fine, at six years of age I thought nothing of it. It was snowing a little bit, in languid flakes. On my head they had put a large cap made of red wool that somehow formed a ruffle around the neck and was tapered to a point at the top. So, Aunt Jeanne and I got underway. When we arrived at the end of rue Jacquet-Droz, I suggested to my aunt, "You could walk up the usual way, by the rue de l'Arsenal, and I will make a little detour by the steps at the end." My aunt had nothing against this. As I climbed up the stairs that ran alongside a kind of storage place for wood, a man came toward me from the top of the stairs. He was small, appeared poor, and limped a bit. He took me by the hand. At first I was really frightened; then he started to look at me and said, "I thought you would come with me; won't you?" With a sense of fear (were you permitted to refuse a poor man anything?), I replied, "No, Sir, but merry Christmas." He immediately let go of my hand; he seemed to me a bit sad. I continued on my way, and in the following days I kept saying over and over again to myself, "Perhaps I should have said yes, but I could not do anything but say no." When I told the story to Aunt Jeanne, she was horrified and forbade me to leave her side.[3] Everything went completely wrong at the Loze sisters'. The pupils had finished eating; entire plates full of meringues were left. They literally forced me to take some. I ate one with the feeling that it would have been much too rude to decline, and, besides, Aunt Jeanne agreed. And I certainly know that I did not want to disobey Maman out of a desire for sweets; rather, I had done

[3] In her dictated autobiography, Adrienne recounts that she later wrote in a very small notebook that she wanted to say yes to the man after all. This caused a storm of indignation in her mother, who found the notebook.

it in order not to offend the "old" ladies. Upon our return I was violently reprimanded by Maman, who immediately asked whether I had eaten anything and learned the whole story about the man. In those days I cried easily, and I had still not succeeded in drying my tears when Maman rang the bell for the Christmas tree.

3. ON THE EVE OF MY CONVERSION[4]

October 29, 1940

It is no longer the days, it is the hours you count, my soul. Still eighty, exactly; you can do what you want; it is eighty and then comes the greatest gift, the one longed for. And you know you are not worthy to receive it, and yet you will accept it, trembling and giving thanks at the same time; and you will try to comprehend, and yet you know it will stream over you so powerfully that there will be no room left for one single question. You will offer yourself; the Church will accept you, but God? To do more than offer yourself is not within your power. You cannot even attempt to be persuasive or to exalt what has been offered. You know how little value it has; you know that there are many offers, and, despite all humility, you cannot give, but only offer prayerfully. The gift that you receive, however, is so great, so overwhelming, and yet you still stand there, continue to offer yourself in all your poverty, and hope.

Nothing is to be overlooked, and this burning sword, which flashes through my heart so painfully that it can barely be endured, is peace. Can you believe that? Until now, peace was not burning and painful for you; you supposed it was gentle and colorless, and that is precisely what it is not. Now you know it; it is hotter than fire and brings

4 Handwritten.

you the most tormenting joy. Will you endure it? And what if your offer is not accepted?

Midnight is already long past; the fire is slowly dying in the fireplace, and you remember that friends and later your husband as well chattered familiarly with you—not only with your soul—but with you in the comfortable armchairs; now they are all gone; you have gotten up once more because it seemed to you that you must not give too many of these—soon only seventy-nine—hours to sleep. But go and pray awhile; you have to give thanks for so much. You may only suspect for how much; but you cannot know, much less give sufficient thanks.

November 1st

Pour aujourd'hui il n'y a qu'un mot, un seul: merci.

Nov. 3. Might I have suspected that everything would be so difficult? Thank God there is no way back; *et s'il existait, je ne le prendrais pas.*

Nov. 4. All Saints: Would that I could relive it, experience the beautiful feast again, completely. A trace of anxiety was also mixed with the great joy. And now, if this unique day could be repeated, that trace would be completely gone. For I experience it every day anew, the strength bestowed on me is so wonderful, so fulfilling. To give a little of this to friends would be a blessing for me; I wonder if precisely this will be granted to me? It is expected, but I am so unworthy, so incapable of achieving what is expected.

4. ADRIENNE ON HER STATEMENTS ABOUT HERSELF

Under obedience to SPN, Adrienne is supposed to make statements about herself. She shrinks greatly from doing so. Nothing is more embarrassing to her than certain descriptions given by the saints about themselves, a number of whom she names.

When I was little I did not want to talk about myself. I knew that a secret was at work in my life, and I guarded it carefully. I cannot understand how the little Thérèse could say of herself that she had not committed a mortal sin: this really should have belonged to her secret and especially to the secrecy of the confessional. For her confessor must have told her this during confession. Just as one does not talk about the sins one has confessed, neither is the opposite intended for publication. The seal of the confessional may primarily concern the confessor, but in a deeper sense the penitent is part of it as well.

There is a sphere of complete discretion: between Father and Son, Christ and the Church, confessor and penitent, husband and wife. After all, what do we know of the relationship of the newborn Christ child to his heavenly Father—but which was surely a relationship of the greatest depth, the richest reciprocity—now that the Son possesses the created mother given him by the Father! Or what do we know of the attitude of Mary, the sinless one, toward the angel before whom she stood in a perfect attitude of confession. The words of the angel to her are like an exhortation after the completed confession, a mission. God may unveil some of such mysteries if he wants to, but much—and maybe most—remains totally veiled.

Adrienne shrinks back, as we see, from making any valid statements about herself, about her complete nakedness before God. She does not want to speak of her nakedness before God the way the little Thérèse speaks of her littleness. This shy reserve can only be overcome under obedience (and even the confessor must obey in commanding). It is an ecclesiastical secret comparable to a confession demanded under obedience. In virtue of this obedience, Adrienne is brought to a specific state that removes from her every possibility of reflection on self. And afterward God can manage things as he wants, shaping her knowledge or ignorance about herself as he pleases.

It is therefore extremely important to keep in mind that almost all the following statements about herself are the fruits of an entirely specific obedience and are indebted exclusively to it.

These statements are quite fragmentary. They cannot and do not intend to replace the two biographies published later. They are only meant to highlight the kind of person Adrienne was. Central things remain unmentioned: her relationship to the triune God, to Christ, to Mary, to the Church.

5. ADRIENNE'S RELATIONSHIP TO DEATH

Before the Conversion. I have never known the fear of death. As a small child, I was often very close to death, but I do not remember this. The earliest that I can still remember is when I was struck by a carriage on January 1, 1911. There was a commotion, and the people thought that I was dead. But the only fear I had was of Maman on account of the red coat. When they said that I could have been dead, it did not strike me as unpleasant at all; it would have been rather nice.

Later on, when I fell into the pond, all I thought was how amazing it is a person could be in the water so long without dying. But I was not overly interested. When I saw the ironing woman who had caught fire, I became aware of the horror of death for the first time. It made such a big impression on me because of the poor ironing woman, not because of me. Afterward I could no longer remember her face, and I was very sad that I had no picture of her.

Then came the deaths of my grandmother and my father. It was sad but not actually terrifying. And it belonged to the world and to the order of the adults; death did not touch me as a problem in those days. But, shortly after the death of my grandmother, a little cousin who was ten months old died. I had seen her only the day before; she lay there unconscious, her eyes half-open. I was told that she was very sick and would possibly die. That irritated me enormously because she looked like a healthy child sleeping, apart from the half-open eyes. And how did the grown-ups know that she was dying? A child is not meant to die! Will she always remain a child in heaven? Or will she become older and reach a kind of adulthood? That would be nice, because the children would then be reared by God himself and would no longer do the silly pranks that we carry on here.

In Langenbruck I was told for the first time that my own death was imminent. At first I was quite amazed that the question could apply to oneself. The doctor said, "You will not be here when spring comes." And now it was around the beginning of September. I thought that maybe I would still make it to May. I could record the remaining days as marks on a piece of paper and cross out one daily. Perhaps the day would finally come when I would be too tired to cross one out; thus by this time death would be very close. But then this method seemed completely disgraceful to me. You would really be occupied with yourself every day, and the whole thing would be like an accusation against God. There are of course a few things that must be done before you die. But they are really only a few. As for the rest, you can simply trust in God and continue to do what has to be done. And for the time being, that means being sick. I accepted the doctor's pronouncement as absolutely certain; I thought it impossible that he could be wrong. I did not experience any anxiety about the moment of transition, nor was I the least bit afraid of hell, either, although I had always believed in it and had a vivid image of it. Only when I converted did I learn that Protestants actually do not believe in hell. For me, hell was this horrible punishment of not being allowed to see God. Dying, however, seemed somewhat like advancing into the next grade in school: you would surely learn something new, something thrilling. When a new teacher arrived in secondary school—I was eleven years old at the time—this was always a tremendous event. I saw what came after death only in a positive light. "Surely there will be something exciting again." And just as you ask the pupils in the higher grades what they are doing now, so I imagined, after you had died, asking the dead what it was like on the other side of judgment. Because, for me, you could look at God from two sides after death: first, the judgment where you will be reproached for various things and where God will somehow teach you what is "customary in heaven". And after that, he will release you to the gracious God. But there will be sufficient time to ask the "departing group" how it was in court. Just as happens during an exam where one group is inside and the others are still waiting in front of the door asking the ones who are leaving how it was. All of this did not make me anxious but, rather, joyful. I had the certain feeling that my God would surely show me everything. Just as a new maid is shown how it is customary to set the table in one's home.

When I was in Leysin, Jeanne Lacroix died. The Catholic prayers for the dying and last sacraments made a deep impression on me: through them one is lifted up to God. She had suffered from terrible headaches; I was told she was hysterical. It was learned only after her death that she had had a brain tumor. From the Waldau and also

Leysin, I was well aware of what hysteria is. I wondered if you could really die of hysteria? Perhaps to make yourself interesting, to spite others? I knew of patients who faked their temperatures, of some who pretended to be severely ill in order to extort some sort of advantage. But Jeanne had never impressed me as hysterical. All of this intrigued me as a problem. Could it possibly happen that somebody acts hysterically, pretends to be sick, and is then suddenly, as though in punishment, taken seriously by God and set upon the downward path to death?

Then there is the question of acknowledging one's own death. What do people usually feel when they know with certainty that they are dying? This coming face to face with death, with the intention and the will of God! How will a person behave toward God when he has followed his own will all his life and now suddenly realizes that he has no other choice but to follow God's road? It was in Leysin that the death of so many other people became a problem for me for the first time.

During medical school: the bodies handed over for dissecting. It seemed absolutely terrible to me before-hand. Having to deal with these bodies for years! I was somehow afraid they might alienate me from life. But, as I actually settled down to work, this fear evaporated. The problem of death did not accompany me into the dissect-ing room. It only surfaced again two years later when I was in contact with living patients. Now it meant help-ing them to die. I felt horrible when the fact that they were dying was concealed from the sick; there would be the whispered "tonight" to the relatives in the hall, and then they would return smiling so the patient would not notice anything. This way he was cheated out of his encounter with God. I always had the sense of a "priv-ileged position" here, or, to put it better, of a mission.

It was with a certain ease that I talked to the people as a student. You had a natural cheerfulness, and, even if you got very little sleep, still you were never tired, or so it seems to me, at least, in retrospect. (And, besides, I was a bit idolized in the hospital, treated with great respect by nurses and patients during the time I was working with Hotz and Staehelin.)

From then on—and all through the years of my medical practice—my relationship to death has not changed. There would probably be something like a purely physical, reflexive fear if you were suddenly told, "In one minute you will be dead." But that has nothing to do with spiritual reflection. And spiritually I never had any fear of death. When I was told in Cassina that I would die that evening, I had time to reflect and was not afraid at all. Or if I were told, "Your next heart attack will be the last", I would not be the least bit afraid. Only a precipitous event might cause fright, as, for example, if a knife were suddenly pulled against me. But that would only be a brief interruption of what is normal: the joy of seeing God soon. But if I knew *in advance* that death were coming now, the reunion with God, then even the drawn knife would not make any impression on me. Later on, every time I suffered a severe heart attack and it seemed to be the end, I was always unbelievably happy that now, finally, the time had come.

I wonder if each vision is not an announcement or an image of death. You go beyond, enter into heaven with the same spiritual, matter-of-fact attitude with which you will cross over completely one day. I could very well imagine that one day I would see the Mother of God and then simply continue to dwell in this vision. And death would thus be characterized by the longer duration of an otherwise familiar vision. You simply dwell in it and, in all this joy and beauty, forget to continue breathing. And all of a sudden you would notice that you had been dead for quite some time and had not even noticed it.

Of course there are also entirely different possibilities: because of a difficulty in breathing, you might sink as if into a dark hole; or you might be led into death slowly, made to experience it in detail, as an experiment, before being returned from there to life.

6. ADRIENNE'S PRAYER AS A SMALL CHILD

As a child I had a definite worry that in the interim between two prayers you could stray from God. Certainly, in a new prayer you can again put straight many things that have gotten a bit out of line. Nevertheless, a child should not rely on prayer to the extent that, in the meantime, he feels free and intentionally strays from God, thinking that, after all, he can return again in the next prayer. A good mother must tell a child, as soon as he has sufficient intelligence and understands his mistakes, that he ought to put things straight before he begins to pray. Just as one goes to confession before he communicates.

Now and then I had fun with other children. When I knew, in doing so, that I could still pray, everything was fine. I went on the most venturesome expeditions in Grandmother's park, and my mind was entirely engaged in play. Yet I did not feel alienated. For instance, I could imagine that I was hiding together with my God. If, however, I had bothered another child while playing, I would have immediately forfeited the feeling of being able to pray, and that is how I recognized that it was wrong. I always had this standard of measure in the background: I noticed that I was alienated from myself when I could not find God just as easily in an activity as I found him, for instance, when starting to pray.

7. THE GROWTH OF CHARITY IN ADRIENNE'S CHILDHOOD

In her youth: It begins with the helplessness of others. Helen is nineteen months older than I am. But I always perceive her as helpless. She is a "little bit" favored by Mother. If one of us is allowed to accompany her, then it is naturally the older one; she may also stay up longer; she gets the new dresses, and so on. But very early I had the feeling that even if she were the older one, still she was more helpless than I was. My life had a kind of richness, and hers, a kind of poverty (to express this in the words of grown-ups). It was as though less were given to Helen. When we were playing with the cow or the horse, for instance, or even with two little stones or blades of grass, I was always completely occupied, never bored. I would braid a crown, for example, from the grass: it was the crown of my God. Or the winner would get the crown when we played "war" with the little stones clashing against each other in battle. Or the blades of grass would become the food for the Lord's sheep. And you had to consider into how many parts to divide it so that all of them would receive something. Or you made soup for everybody out of it. This is how it was. But Helen was invariably finished with the game and needed something more, something new. She was helpless. Everything had to be explained to her: "No, a stone really isn't a king", she would say. So I left all the real toys to her, not at all by virtue of a "renunciation", but more from a sense of justice and maybe of love.

Later on, there were the patients in Father's office. There was one with a bandaged eye. I always felt then like wearing a bandage over my eye, also. I thought it might perhaps console him if someone else had something similar, particularly the doctor's child. For some time I earnestly wanted to be blind because I thought that another child who was blind would, in the meantime, be able to see. The first of March was the canton's festival commemorating the entrance of the canton, Neuchâtel, into the Swiss Confederation. My father said that there were always accidents; the children injured themselves so easily with the fireworks. I asked Father if I could be the child that got hurt this year. I thought that the child could simply be chosen and then some other accident would be prevented. I somehow believed that God probably had to have a child and that, if one offered himself, the others would be saved. I was four or five years old at the time.

I also wanted to help those who limped and anyone who had to walk with a cane. And, since the blind played such an important part at our place, I was always on the lookout to see if I could help one across the street. A triumph if it happened to be two or three! And then, to carry baskets! Eternally! I offered my help to the most robust women who were lugging their baskets. From the point of view of the adults, it was completely ridiculous. The number of baskets *I* have carried! I thrived on the idea that helping has an *aftereffect*, and all my life I have felt happy when *I* received help myself. That produces community. I was always very much afraid the others might be lonely. When I help them—so I thought—they are less alone. I did not want to talk to them because you cannot cure loneliness by talking. But when I was carrying a basket—now I see them again before my eyes, these market baskets, covered with kerchiefs, and all the things they contained!—then I felt intimately connected with the people. And I talked to God about the owner of the basket up to the moment when we reached the doorstep.

Then the matter had come to an end and the person could now live a little bit on this. The thought that I had done "a good deed" did not enter my head for a moment. Everything was always done quickly and with finality. You felt happy only when you were doing the carrying because you had the feeling that it was something meaningful. You no longer thought of it afterward.

During the school years all of this continues; as long as I was in La Chaux-de-Fonds, I carried baskets. Later, when I was a big girl, I would not have dreamed of offering my help to a woman who was effortlessly walking along with her basket.

I often felt the helplessness of my classmates, too. And this I have never confessed: that in school I cheated so incredibly ... in order to do written assignments for others. Simply because they were so helpless. In elementary school I did a good deal of prompting; I was good at that. But in secondary school I did a lot of written assignments for others. I was simply much farther ahead than the others; as strange as it might sound today, I was an excellent pupil. Everything came easy to me. The pupils were intentionally separated in the classroom in such a way that no one could cheat. Nevertheless, pages and notebooks could be smuggled across. I was always finished well before the others, and so I helped them. I could not have cared less that what I did was punishable. And, after all, what is punishment when you know that others are unhappy or when they say, "My father will thrash me if I ..." Horrible! And that is how I came to love *very much* everybody in school. Because in everybody I saw some helplessness. And if someone was sick, I was very unhappy.

I learned to love the grown-ups much later than the children, except when I could detect a helplessness in them as well. The market women! But my grandmother's friends and the committeewomen who had tea with my mother did not interest me at all. They lived in a world that was inaccessible to me, one in which I was not *needed*. My love was always, in the first place, an answer to a need I had perceived.

Personal friendships? Madeleine. The reason, because together we wanted to convert Madeleine Junod. Willy, because he was paralyzed. Teddy, because he was still just a small child when we were already half-grown. I was ten and a half when he was born.

I loved my father's patients very much at that time when I knew that they were ill. Otherwise, if I could not tell that they were sick by looking at them, I was hardly interested. But when I saw, in the hospital, that they had bandaged eyes or glass eyes—those glass eyes were horrible!—then I loved them. Then I would have wished to spend a life of love in their midst. Once I thought that would be a mission, going through the hospital wards all day long with glasses of tea, and each one who was thirsty would immediately have the opportunity to drink. And, because I myself was sick so much, I knew how it is when you are in bed and nobody thinks of you. (When I had pneumonia in 1932, they forgot to bring me anything to eat for three days; everybody was so terribly agitated. That was, as it were, the "crowning" of my being thirsty a lot as a child. Emil did not notice that I was supposed to be drinking and the servant girl, Anna Bürglin, was crying all day.) Or I would run a temperature at night, and Mother would say, "I won't bring you anything to eat, only something to drink"; then I would hear how they were having dinner in the next room, the children at six, the grown-ups at seven. And then Mother would forget about it, and I would be completely parched, having waited for a glass of water all afternoon.

And then in school: I always took the punishment for the others upon myself. Almost as a sport. So the teachers no longer believed that it had been I. There was a limit only when the boys' lavatory was involved; I did not raise my hand when something had happened there.

In the Waldau: all those crying and screaming people. My uncle would send me through the ward somewhat like a medication. You could soothe the sick, start conversations with them, and draw their attention to something new. Such a little girl knows how to approach even the insane. You "roll" into this in a way, and somehow the ball is pushed onto the right track. The feeling of being able to *take* something of the sick *upon myself* was much less pronounced in the Waldau; I had it only when I was in church and with those who were screaming. Invariably, at least one patient would scream in church. The thought would occur to me every time: Could I not be together with her in her sadness?

A tremendous impression was made on me by my uncle, who knew every one of his one thousand one hundred patients by name and greeted every new arrival personally; who did not shrink from driving criminals unaccompanied to the penitentiary in Witzwil. Helen was Aunt Jeanne's favorite, and I was my uncle's. When he said, "my Niessli", all was right with the world. Only in geography did he find me very weak. How often he would stand with me by the window early in the morning and ask me the names of mountains and places. This weakness has remained with me. I do not know the stars at all. I was always very poor in history. I think I was too preoccupied with my more immediate surroundings, with people. On walks, as a small child, I never knew my way. I had simply run along with the others, and, besides, I was probably too intensely occupied with the angels. A lot of things in my life were, in fact, arranged so that I did not have to worry about them.

In the Waldau my love for the sick became somehow definitive; and my interest in medicine as well. My father, my uncle, and De Quervain were the impressive men during my youth; all three were physicians. But everything was ruled by the thought that when a patient is helped, he will be happy again. How anxious I was every time Father operated on a blind patient and the operation was known to be dangerous. A direct line led from here to the patients who were exhibited like merchandise and often almost offered for sale in the university lecture halls, to the patients in the hospital wards, and finally to my own patients.

8. DEVELOPMENT OF THE RELATIONSHIP BETWEEN LOVE OF GOD AND LOVE OF NEIGHBOR IN ADRIENNE'S YOUTH

1. There was a time in my life—approximately between my sixth and eighth year—when I drew a distinct dividing line between children and adults. There were no thirteen- to eighteen-year-olds in my environment at that time. And grown-ups impressed me as mysterious beings who live according to entirely different laws, have different reactions, and, on the whole, live much more pleasantly than children. This kind of life intrigued me greatly for I almost had the feeling that they were as if in a bowl, and the content of this bowl was life. And they take just what they want from this bowl; they take their happiness and their sadness, their work, their relaxation, and joy. But even if they can choose what they want from it quite arbitrarily, they can, nevertheless, choose nothing other than

what God has put into their bowl. Someone may very well be able to choose to be happy or sad; but not *this* kind of sadness or *that* kind of joy. It was through my own experience that I hit upon this thought: when I had fallen once and hurt my knee, I could indeed choose to scream or not to scream, but I could not choose to scream because of a different pain than the one in my knee. Only I thought that adults somehow have a greater range, a greater selection than children. And I thought they would see much more of God's mystery than children.

One time a deranged woman—she was from a good family—came to see my father. She had been brought into the parlor. For some reason I went in. The woman was talking with her voices without feeling disturbed by me. I thought that perhaps she was talking to God. I was convinced, however, that even as children we are living in God, only we are not able to discern it. The grown-ups tell you, "Go to bed now." I have to obey because I am too little to follow God directly. And it is somehow clear to me that the grown-ups who are giving me the order have settled this matter in their own way with God, that the command proceeds not only from their authority, but comes directly from God.

Thus, even at that time, I was unable to distinguish between love of neighbor and love of God. I love the children in God; that means that they enlarge my love of God because they magnify the mystery, the feeling that we are a bunch of stupid little children who are too simple to be able to recognize God's commands. But then I am *touched* that we are still protected and loved by God despite our simple-mindedness. I feel a kind of community of simple-mindedness, of childlikeness, that heightens my love toward God. All of us are standing together before him, and you understand as little as I do.

And we talk about God in Sunday School or on a walk; but perhaps I am the only one who is telling something about God. Then I sometimes think that perhaps the others are not saying anything because they know so much more than I do. Most likely I am behind them in my knowledge and love of God. But it could also be that they know less. In any case, there is a discretion here: one must not insist. It is all right to pester the maid to death to tell me the story of Little Red Ridinghood for the hundredth time. But I must never pester anybody to tell me about God. And somehow it does not make any difference to me whether the others know more or less than I do. I would be inclined to maintain that both are true at once—more and also less. For as a child I considered this "more" to be an invitation and not at all a demand. I do not sense at all that my God *demands* that I know him more and more; rather everything is somehow good as it is. The discrepancy that will arise later does not exist at all at this age. Later on I will become aware that God is different and that I must strive to understand his being-different. As a child, your relationship to God is clouded only when you have done "something foolish".

2. There was also a time when I was rarely sent to my grandmother's without returning after five or ten minutes with skinned knees. That was when I was between seven and nine years old. I was sick a lot, very skinny, had grown considerably, and was obviously extremely clumsy. I fell down constantly. I never looked where I was going. I flew off, looking at the sky. And so I would trip over the first curb and fall down in the street. I was admonished, "Watch where you are going! Pay attention." It is no use; the next moment I fall down again. Then, each time, my father would bandage my knees after he had put on iodine.

It always seemed to me that God would have to do it. He would have to live and stay within me. For I was not capable of doing this alone. I was not clumsy when I had homework or some specified task to carry out. But when I was given a whole afternoon off for "thinking",[5] then I was somehow completely "deluged" interiorly by the freedom I now had in God. We were really kept so strictly at home; we were awfully well brought up: always clean fingernails, ribbons in our hair, moderate in speech, no loud laughter. We had to be terribly good. And I had such a hard time being good. When I was finally free, I did not feel like making a lot of noise, for instance, but interiorly I was like a whirlwind. At two o'clock, I am dismissed and told, "Go to Grandmother." And now, four hours free! On my way, I tell trees and clouds that I am free now. At my grandmother's, you do not need to think expressly of God. You simply *are* with him; you are looking at him. And you are free to look at him as you will. At home there are continual interruptions: "Adrienne, tenez-vous droite! Adrienne, why are you so quiet?" There is constant fault-finding. At Grandmother's, you are left totally in peace. The new governess is even worse than the former ones, "Adrienne, je vous rends attentive au fait que vous ne vous tenez pas droite." And yet, when she left, I cried as seldom before—because I had a bad conscience for not having loved her. I had the feeling God would demand her soul from me on Judgment Day! She was horrid, white hair and eyes that protruded from her head. And she ate up absolutely everything we received as a present. She was also an expert at rousing a bad conscience in us, the Mademoiselle Fischer. She knew how to make a "production" out of the

[5] About this "thinking", her childlike manner of contemplation, see *Das Geheimnis der Jugend* (The mystery of youth), vol. 7 of the posthumous works.

most trivial matters, and because this was so tiresome to me I just gave her my things—chocolate and the like—in order to "silence" her.

The relationship to my God was a little disturbed at that time. First, because he does nothing to prevent me from falling down. Secondly, because he does not make Mademoiselle Fischer less disgusting. And thirdly, because Mademoiselle Fischer is full of stories about people who are poor, all of whom she knows personally. Therefore it seems to me that God ought to care for these people a little better. That is why there is now a difference from before: God is now the same God for the grown-ups as for the children. Grown-ups also have the same possibility of not understanding everything.

And when I am about twelve years old, I have the intense feeling that God is simply different. It is not his fault. But neither is it because of sin on our side. Rather, somewhere there is an elementary non-correspondence. And you know that surely there must be people who know how you can correspond to God. But they do not say it loudly enough. And from this moment on, all the questions of people, their destinies, their sorrows, become pointers to God, become ways that run in his direction. They are exponents of the love and power of God and of his demands. Everything is an incentive to search for God. This search is the new thing in my life. It is evident that God wants to live in unity with us. It is further evident that we must do something so that this joy, this harmony can come about. All of us, I, you, he. Some, however, are privileged: I am among the children whom God allows to think of him a lot. Thus the sense of obligation arises. For, if we who are privileged to pray do not pray for the others and draw them along, what then are the others to do, those who have heard nothing about him, who know nothing about him? The sense of responsibility has awakened.

There are the poor people for whom I try terribly hard to win my relatives' sympathies so that they might give me something for them. But then at night during my evening prayers there is a kind of sadness that belongs to the night. As if there were an opposition between day and night. During the day I tried to solicit support in order to get something—money or clothes or something like that. (But I was loath to bring it to the poor myself; only if I absolutely had to.) But, when I was praying at night, these clothes and this food seemed to me entirely secondary. What this poor person needs is prayer, and all the other poor people need it as well.

3. Then there are times when I feel very strongly at certain moments that God loves us. This is a certitude that can completely overpower me at times. And what is overpowering is solely God's love, which cannot be mistaken for anything else. But then when you want to translate it, when you want to communicate it, it bursts like a soap bubble. As if there were nothing to hold it together. As if it were a vision with which nobody knows what to do because nobody sees it, and I cannot lend others my eyes, and no translation seems to me to succeed. Only when I come to be a Catholic will the soap bubble no longer burst; it continues to exist in the same colors, and it is then as if it had become possible to translate and communicate it through the Eucharist. As long as I was searching and knew for sure that somewhere something was false—that the final truth was missing—the happiness I had in my God was fleeting. I knew of this joy, to be sure, and was allowed to experience it again and again. But you could not make it stand still, and there were many days and months when nothing

of it could be "saved". It remained a memory into which even slight doubts were mixed at times—about whether all of this had not been an illusion. And the realization became stronger and stronger: I myself would have to do something, change something, so that this love of God would become permanent in me and through me, so that it would become a reality in me—or even a reality at all in the world.

Without the Eucharist, but also without confession, our knowledge of God's love remains very incomplete. For these are the tangible gifts he has given us. It is terribly hard to talk with a person about God's love if you cannot point to a concrete sign of this love. States and events of the soul are not sufficient. Without confession and the Eucharist, I cannot make you enthusiastic about God. But perhaps I can show you in some measure what confession and the Eucharist mean to me. If you are Protestant, for example, and do not recognize exactly what the Catholic sacraments are, you nevertheless could sense in me that something definite existed even if I could not explain it to you. You should be able to perceive that after my conversion something has changed fundamentally in my life. The power of the sacraments surely ought to become visible in us.

The tormenting thought, "It is different!", which always haunted me before I was Catholic, can in no way be mistaken for the "gap" [*Loch*].[6] Even the source of irritation is completely different in each case. For the non-Catholic, there is an exasperation in the realization, "It is different!", which is not found in the Catholic "gap".

After my conversion, love of neighbor took on a completely different fullness, constancy, evenness. The character of the "soap bubble" had disappeared. And everything

[6] Adrienne calls the experience of mystical abandonment by God "*Loch*", gap.

became much more independent of me than before. Now the will, the readiness of the Church are felt very strongly. And it is the Church who says yes to the present mission; since I belong to the Church, this kind of mission no longer belongs at all to my personal preference but to her. And it makes no difference if some Catholic outsiders say no to it. There is a peace and magnitude in the fullness of the mission. The apostolate now takes part in objective religion. You really do not convert primarily for yourself but, rather, just as much for others.

To be sure, there are still—as earlier with the "soap bubble"—moments when God causes a sense of deep personal joy. But now that it is above all a matter of doing what God wants—even if you no longer see the direction from the outset—you experience a peaceful knowledge of God that is entirely objective and matter of fact and need not at all be especially marked by joy. And you know that this matter-of-fact love can also be given as a gift, and you try to do it in a matter-of-fact way.

This objectivity had already dawned on me to some degree during the years at the university and in my medical practice. In those days, by caring for the sick and simply by my womanly work in general, I tried to do something substantial for my neighbor, out of love for God and in order to bring my neighbor closer to him. But somehow I was timid and careful not to speak of God as the giver of all gifts because I simply knew too little about him. It is true that I had a knowledge of God, but principally that he was different and greater; and I did not want to force my personal bit of knowledge upon others. As a child and as a teenager, I tried to convert everybody who came near me. But then the question arose: To which God? If he is indeed different and greater, I must not nail down another person's faith to my image of God.

This hesitation came to an end when I became a Catholic. Now the mission outweighed my personal opinions. And within the mission you can speak of God much more objectively. And you live from the faith of the Church, who knows much more than the individual believer. And consequently you also have many more points of contact with others as a basis for speaking to them.

9. ADRIENNE AND HOLY SCRIPTURE

As a child, I spent a lot of time with the Bible, but I read it chiefly as a book of stories. We had children's books with titles like *Jésus, l'ami des enfants* and *Les plus belles histoires de l'Ancien et du Nouveau Testament.* I was never very fond of the Old Testament stories; they were as if disconnected, having no real ending. I found the sacrifice of Isaac atrocious, for example. The God of the Old Testament was such a bloodthirsty God! But I read *Jesus, the Friend of Children* innumerable times, very, very slowly, at a time when I was already devouring books as a rule. I think that for a long time I associated a kind of devotion with this book. I was about eight years old then and was already reading prodigiously, but in the evening, before going to bed—usually before dinner, since afterward I had to go directly to bed—I read a little more of it each time, a sentence, a word.

And my grandmother also had a curious way of telling me stories about the Lord. One day she would tell the story of Little Red Ridinghood; the next day, a story from the Bible, whatever happened to be the case—a distinction was not noticeable. She had a very deliberate way of telling a story; her stories were always very "populated". She was devout, had a piety that was perhaps not unlike mine; but she did not in any way display that she was pious. If someone did something foolish, she would never take offense; but, when something was potentially serious, then she would try to point out that the Lord would be offended by it.

When I was little—four and a half, five, six years old—I was very anxious to spend the afternoon alone at Grandmother's from one-thirty to six o'clock. I had my "nest" there, as it were, a corner for myself. She would say that it was certainly permissible for me to be alone, it was certainly all right with her, but still one always belonged to God, and, since one did not see God, one therefore belonged to the people who are his creatures. If you invited children, for example, it would not do to leave them by themselves; at most, you could do so only if you knew that all were entertained. Then I asked her if it were permissible to play hide and seek and to hide yourself in such a way that no one could find you. After all, the others would then be occupied, too. She answered, "Would you like to look all afternoon for somebody who had hidden himself so well that he could not be found?" Whatever Grandmother said or whatever stories she told, it was never boring to be with her.

Aunt Jeanne also read us stories from the Bible; there were pictures in it, and those from the Old Testament were especially beautiful. But she never made any applications but rather left the book to us afterward and showed us the pictures. In Grandmother's book, as well as in Aunt Jeanne's, I somehow learned contemplation by looking at the pictures.

Only after the death of my grandmother did I read Scripture properly for the first time. I was eleven years old. I acquired a Bible for the first time, the one that Grandmother had bequeathed to Helen or to both of us. It was printed in very large letters, and I felt these large letters to be essential for the Bible. For some time after that, Helen and I read something from this Bible in the evening. Grandmother's favorite verse was, "If I have not love, I am nothing." This is why I often read the letter to the Corinthians. For about six months, the Bible was my main reading material; I had put the children's books aside meanwhile. But actually I think I read only the letter to the Corinthians over and over again, and, if I am not mistaken, was forbidden to read the other books. My Bible reading was quite satisfying at that time, surely because it so strongly evoked my grandmother.

This went on until about the summer of 1914. During the next six months, however, until about November, I started to read all of the New Testament, very unsystematically, that is. And this was a real torture, for I always had the feeling that something was not right; it was simply different. It was also the time when I contradicted Pastor Junod time and again during religion class. Junod considered me something of a "holy child", and once, down in Grandmother's garden where there was a mailbox, he told me that he was wondering whether I was to become the proof for him that the Catholic Church was the right one. (I recall this story only now as I see the place in my mind.) I merely laughed and did not know what to make of it; the whole thing seemed incredibly strange to me, since at that time I really did not in the least think at all that to be Catholic meant anything.

The unsystematic reading lasted until around the time of Helen's confirmation on Pentecost of 1917. What I now recount happened at that time. After the group instruction and before confirmation, every child goes individually to meet with the pastor for what is called *le quart d'heure*. It was my opinion that something terrifically important and decisive must happen there, so decisive, I thought, that you would come back completely converted. I also thought that it was a great secret and that one was not to talk about it. When Helen returned from her *quart d'heure*, she was not in the least converted. And, since I saw that, a few days later I dared to refer to the secret and asked her how it had been. At first she acted terribly mysterious, but after that she spoke freely. The pastor had told her that one should act throughout one's life in accord with what had been heard during the class, and he asked whether she knew how babies came into the world and whether she had any other questions to ask him. I was extremely disappointed. I said to myself, "The pastor is even going to spoil the whole Bible for me this way." I laid aside my Bible reading and decided that I would therefore simply communicate with God alone.

Pastor Junod made one other foolish mistake. At the time of the *quart d'heure*, he used to pay a visit to the child's parents and ask them what kind of impression they had of the child. Thus he also came to Maman and told her that he had been so pleased with Helen; she was such a pious child, no wonder she had such a sister. Maman was greatly offended by this, and naturally I was, too. Once more I had the feeling that pastors only spoil things for you.

In Leysin, I picked up the Bible now and then—apart from the idiotic religion class—but most of the time I read only a little from wherever I happened to open it. I somehow started doing this when I ran out of material for prayer.

Later, during medical school, I tried once more to read the New Testament. I would have liked to know more, understand more, be able to quote more for the patients. The feeling haunted me that I lacked the right key to the whole. Scripture was quite all right, but I did not know how to unlock it. Much later—between 1936 and 1939—I once more read a little in the Old Testament, but without much pleasure; for the thought kept recurring: someday I will see the light. And the New Testament was closed to me because of the problem with the Our Father. I no longer remember what I read; but I do know that I was not enlightened by it. Rarely would I read a whole book because I remained totally in the dark. I would read for a quarter of an hour at times, but it seemed rather meaningless to me. Certainly David was a brave man; certainly Solomon was wise, and the prophets were shrewd and capable. But I did not find God. Actually, you can read the Old Testament properly only in the light of the New Testament—as promise. And it was precisely this which was completely lacking.

After my conversion and before I got started on *John*, I read Holy Scripture only in the missal; but I did so very frequently. I cannot remember having read a Gospel before John. The Old Testament continued to frighten me at first, as it had previously. I no longer tried my luck with it except for the Psalms. I was familiar with those from the breviary; but in the breviary I read only the Psalms, not the other texts. In the winter of 1945, I read at least one psalm from Holy Scripture every morning and, in 1946, whole, continuous sections of the Old Testament. At the time of my conversion, I had read the First Letter to the Corinthians once again, but nothing else by Paul. Nor did I read the Apocalypse. I read Mark when I gave the community points for meditation from it.

In the days when I was no longer able to pray the Our Father, I tried once or twice to read the Apocalypse but was seized by a dreadful terror and immediately closed it again and have never reopened it since I became Catholic. I have never read the Acts of the Apostles.

On the whole, I always did know that Scripture is God's Word. But I did not find the right access to it. For I always thought that I did not have the key. Today it is clear to me that the words sound somehow different, depending on whether they are read from a Catholic or a Protestant point of view.

And since I started work on the commentaries, I have read very little in Scripture. I have to remain open for God. I do not want to be like a bride who reads all kinds of love stories in order to learn how to receive her bridegroom. I do not want to forestall God. He should be able to show me what he wants. I feel a kind of veto here. I know very well that every word in Scripture is directed to me—as to each person. But, when I am beginning a commentary, I need to be very much alone with God in order to be able to come from him, as it were, in approaching the book that is to be interpreted.

10. HELD IN RESERVE

Adrienne recounts several additional details at the end of her written biography.

She remembers having known very clearly during her later childhood, in the *Gymnasium* years, that "something is going to happen." At the same time, in such moments, she knew: I must keep myself in readiness, but it will not come forth from myself. And there are certain things that I simply *cannot* do; and even if I should strive to do them, I would be prevented from it. There was a definite knowledge of the impossibility of committing "this sin", and that this impossibility did not depend on her, was not "her achievement". During her school years, she knew quite precisely what she could do and what she could not. In certain things that the class as a whole did, she knew the limit: *I* cannot do it. And this was not even from a feeling of responsibility toward God. When the teacher asked afterward, "Who did it?" Adrienne would say, without reflection or scruple, "I did it!" Of course in doing so, she knew that the teacher would not believe her. Yet not one single time did he say, "It is not true", but, rather, dealt the punishment with a smile.

A small incident: one time when she was between twelve and fourteen years old—it was in the lower *Gymnasium*—she was standing on a furnace outlet from which warm air was blowing, puffing up her skirt. The teacher came by and gave her a thorough scolding: this was quite improper. Adrienne did not at all understand why. But in the midst of this lack of comprehension, she knew that there are things like this that "one" must not do although one cannot see why not. In the future, I must not stand in places that make my skirt look like a balloon. And that applies to girls in general. But perhaps it is the something "different"—set apart—that accounts for the fact that I do not understand it. One is being saved for something. She had then forgotten this story very quickly.

The feeling of "being saved for something" continues. In the final days before her first marriage, it makes itself felt quite acutely; but it is clearly present at other times as well, even during her marriage. It was very evident when her father died in La Chaux-de-Fonds. Adrienne had already wept in the room; now she was weeping at the front door. And at the same time, she knew, "In my personal loss I must not behave as if I did not have the strength to go on living because as yet I have not even begun what will one day be expected of me. What I do know is that the family is counting on me. Though things will never work out with Maman and me. But I *must* be the one in the family to whom they can go." "In this moment of my youth", Adrienne said, "I saw far ahead. And it was not as though everything depended on me but, rather, that

I had to remain and walk in a prescribed direction that was unknown to me but in which one day something was going to happen.

"This whole matter is completely different from the resolutions you make about what you want to become and achieve in life. In school when we talked together about our future plans and the boys would ask me, '*Et toi?*', I certainly talked very big. A huge hospital, and so on. And yet in the back of my mind I knew at the same time that I would never carry it out; it would never work because I had to do 'something different'. Yet that never kept me from describing my hospital at great length, whereas I could never say a word about that something else. And this was not at all because I was too embarrassed to talk about it but, rather, because this whole area was simply entirely set apart."

11. A CONVERSATION WITH THE FIFTEEN-YEAR-OLD

Adrienne explains to me: Whenever I want to do something bad, a voice comes to me from outside to prevent me from doing so. And it is not the voice of my conscience.

She tells me about her penitential exercises. She pinches herself. She steps on her own feet. She does not take medicine when she is sick. She "does that for the poor" because she has nothing else for them.

She asks me, "Are you afraid, too? Now and then I am afraid while I am praying." "Of what?" *I ask.* "I am not afraid alone. I am afraid together with somebody. But when I express it like this, it is not quite true. For I only see one part of the thing. I am not afraid of somebody but of 'something'. He, the other, sees the whole. I see only a little section. Perhaps it is because I am so fearful that I see only a small part." "Say 'yes' to your fear", *I say*. Adrienne continues, "You know, teachers always say that we are awful *raisonneurs*. But I am not a *raisonneuse*. I can leave things as they are. Or better, not *I* can; it is like a demand. I do not know how to say it. When I pray, 'Forgive us our trespasses as we ...' that would be a tremendous thing. To be so disposed that we could forgive everybody. There are many of us who pray like this, maybe a hundred thousand, maybe ten million. But there are many who would doubtless like very much to be forgiven but who do not themselves forgive. They do not even dream of doing so. And when I am praying this, I am often *afraid of precisely this*. But I know that I see only a very small part. And if I were a *raisonneuse*, I would try to investigate the whole thing properly. I would also ask many people, 'Do you *really* want to forgive?' And if I saw that they were not doing so, then I would *know* that I was afraid because of these particular people. But precisely this I am unable to do. I have to leave everything as it is."

12. CERTAINTIES

Throughout all my life—particularly between 1920 and 1930—there have been things that did not appear to be supernatural at all but that were surrounded by a certainty for which I could not have offered any rational arguments. I suddenly knew things by which I could guide myself, things of which I had perhaps had no idea a moment before, things I had never imagined but that were fully developed the moment they surfaced. Often they seemed to be quite insignificant things. I would be going through the hospital wards, and suddenly I had to go back to a patient and say just that one word which he needed that day. Then if the patient replied, "O thank God that you said that. I was quite desperate", and so on, then I did not know whether the patient wished to be polite or if this were really true. I never reflected about this in detail because I knew that in such things there is an admonition not to reflect. In reflecting, you begin to draw things from the other world into the natural one. You deprive the things, and perhaps yourself, of a meaning that may exist but that is not meant to be explored. You destroy something that requires protection. There are things that remain intact only in their spontaneity; they must be left as they are.

During my childhood, when I was in fourth grade, I was once standing in a corner with a girl. And I was busy consoling her. In the afternoon I had the feeling that I should console her still more; I brought an entire schoolbag full of things from home that I wanted to give her without attracting any attention. I did not know at all why I was doing this. But—as one is very likely to do at that age—I had promised the girl an abundance of divine consolations. And so that she would believe this, I wanted to bring her an abundance of human consolations as well. After recess, the teacher asked me why I had been standing in the corner like that with the girl. "To console her", I said. "What for?" I did not know. "What did you talk about?" "About God." "Very well, but what has this girl confided to you?" "Nothing special" (in fact, she had said nothing at all). The teacher said, "*Ah, alors un ange a passé.*" She meant to say that it was probably an inspiration. You did something inspired by an angel, without noticing how right it was. Only much later, when I was already working in the hospital, did that teacher's statement come back to me. (Incidentally, I learned afterward that this girl had been abused by her father. I learned this from my father, who had to prepare some sort of expert opinion for the court. The teacher also knew about this, and when Father told me about it, he expressed himself very delicately: that father had treated the girl like his wife. At the time I did not really comprehend what he meant.) The expression about the angel remained with me: what is in reality taking place you leave to the realm of the unknown. I probably did not remember at the time having talked to my guardian angel in my early youth.

Later I knew with certainty, but in a way that defied precise definition, that the Lord gives you something like "hints". He somehow shows you that here and there you ought to help a little. It would be complicated if he had to reveal himself; perhaps faith is not strong enough there, or else there is some obstacle. Nor would it be quite right if the pastor came with a Bible verse or the sister with a holy card. Rather, it is better to go there with a small remark, as on an errand, a little mission that is included within the Lord's great one. Then you bring to the suffering ones something that truly comes from God, something that conveys to them the idea that they have not been forsaken by God but that can be achieved without special *éclat* and trouble. It also means, for me, nothing complicated, nothing particularly forceful; it is simply contained within a greater obligation. And it is like a small sign that one is not left entirely alone. Like when someone has a slight temperature all the time and thinks to himself that he should go for an examination some day; you ought to know what is actually causing the fever.

At times things of that sort also happened at the hospital. For example, there were patients who did not seem to be critically ill but who died the following night. Perhaps you knew in advance that they would die, or perhaps you did not even know it, but, in any case, you still had to go to them and prepare them a little for God; you had to talk with them a little about God. Soon afterward they became unconscious, or they did not wake up from their sleep, or they suffered a stroke.

13. THE THREE GREAT GRACES OF HER LIFE

During the spiritual exercises in Kerns, in 1947, I ask Adrienne what she considers to be the greatest mysteries in her life. She answers:

1. *The great mystery of childhood and youth.* That it was made clear to me time and again that I was being set apart, held in reserve for something. At certain moments there was the knowledge that it was one of God's mysteries for which you had to be ready, and, along with it, there was a strong sense of his protection. How much sin was around me, I did not know at all; I only learned it later. In this there were two points of emphasis: first, being held in reserve in the physical sense, then the Mother of God as companion, especially after the vision. And I knew that she had revealed something of her mystery then, but not so that I should investigate it further. There was some sort of obedience involved. After all, I was an alert child who posed endless questions and wanted to get to the bottom of everything—the more I really came into contact with life, as in Leysin. But *la pureté de la vie* was so pervasive a gift that it can only be explained by the Mother of God together with obedience, that the mystery is to be allowed to stand without questions.

Today, on account of the mission, you can make me remember and forget what you wish. A beginning lay in the vision of the Mother: through her I learned to live in what was given (by God), not to search for or think

about what was not given; and all of this as yet name-
less and undefined. This whole experience of being protected stood framed, as it were, between the two visions
of SPN and the Mother. I was also "burdened" with
various sufferings at that time that were to be accepted
without reflecting and were an initiation into the present;
such were the Good Fridays of my youth, which were not
active penitential exercises but, rather, had to be accepted
as sufferings. These were God's demands, quite in keeping
with my age at the time.

2. Something else that was related to this was *the endless
search for God*, above all from the time of Sunday School
and catechism. The absolute knowledge that something
was not right there: it must be different. An emergence of
the Catholic from all sides. And the attempt to lead a life
that would correspond to this as yet unknown demand.
Later in medical school and married life: always the search
for God. At the sea in Caslano: contemplation of God;
times when I deliberately dwelled on a question, a theme,
laid bare the place within myself until I understood something. The many churches visited in Italy and the prayers
in them. Then Emil's death and the question about the
meaning of death arising with it: all of this embedded in
the one search for God, the uneasy knowledge that "it is
different." And time and again being thrown back away
from God; as if I were looking at a mass of problems from
the wrong angle. I sensed that very distinctly. Each time I
thought I was breaking through, I was then thrown back
again to the starting point, where a new question arose.
All of this was probably a preparatory grace, for afterward
I was able to run the faster. In the midst of this, the role of
Pastor Cavallieri, the apostate Catholic priest in Leysin, in
whom it was evident that the greatest sin is to have known
God and then to have forgotten him.

3. *The conversion and the graces it contained.* The long path from childhood had been preparation and now acquired its meaning. I had lived as though in front of a locked room, had set up my furniture in the hallway and kept it as clean as possible. Thus God had prepared everything for the moment I would move in, for the moment also of the vision, and so on. The appearance of SPN and the Mother in my youth were a "pre-vision", a *pledge*, as it were, so I would not despair, and also so that I would persist in a kind of obedience (this was especially so in the case of the Mother of God). The decisive moment in my conversion occurred when you told me, "Pray the entire Our Father." What you were actually saying was: Do not count on your ability but on grace. You cannot make a pact with God: "What I say to you in prayer I can also keep, and what I cannot keep, neither will I say." This was the great turning point: the elimination of the self. At the same time it was the true preparation for the reception of the sacraments; directly from there the way was opened to baptism, to confession, and to Communion. The I that receives the sacraments is not at all the I that I think I am.

14. THE MANNER OF PRAYER BEFORE CONVERSION

1. *When I was little,* I had a kind of prayer that always accompanied me, even though it certainly did not always have the same intensity. It was like a climbing plant that was wound first around this part, then around that part of the soul. You felt surrounded by it. There were corners where it clung tightly; then again, others where this was less so, and others where this was more so. At times it was the thought of God or of a poor person; then again it was an intention, a joy, a sadness, but always within prayer. It was not a "mood", but an accompaniment. The recited

prayer formulas, the Protestant ones, definitely annoyed me. On big occasions, but quite seldom, my father prayed a child's prayer with us in this way. I did not understand a word of it. What we learned to pray in Sunday School also annoyed me. I liked to listen to the Bible stories that they told us. But I could not follow along with the prayer, I learned the *Notre Père* somewhat mechanically, by ear; for example, I never understood what "*saucieu*" meant (*vous êtes aux cieux*). "*Und segne, was Du uns bescheret hast*"[7] I understood for the first time when I was twenty. And since I did not understand anything, I tried to pray properly only at night after the lights were out. Nothing came then, either, of my attempt to repeat mechanically the prayers of the grown-ups. What succeeded was a kind of contemplation: I would, for example, repeat the words *Notre Père* over and over, picturing the Father, heaven, and the angels and the throne from which he sees everything that happens on earth, and then, together with him, I too sought to see all men, particularly the negroes; the negroes played an important role. I would imagine how the cloud of God descended to earth and was a little afraid of being just in that spot and of being overwhelmed by it. I could not imagine the child Jesus at all, but Jesus as friend of children I could picture very well. It remained like this until I was around eight or ten years old.

Later the idea developed that the earth was being lifted into heaven. Grandmother had died, and I thought that, just as she had done, so all other dying people would bring a portion of the earth into heaven with them. For I could never imagine that heaven and earth were two worlds; they had to be one.

---

[7] From a German table grace: "And bless what you have bestowed on us."
— TRANS.

2. *During my marriage with Emil.* The last great storm of prayer before my conversion occurred perhaps in the last days before my marriage. In prayer I put up a fierce resistance, with everything I had, with my whole personality. I had a horrible fear that everything would be wrong and I would no longer be able to breathe; or if I could breathe, I would be a different person than I was, and all the intentions of God that I thought were in some manner in harmony with my own would be smothered.

At the beginning of my marriage, I was wretchedly unhappy until about 1931, and my prayer was completely changed. To be sure, I prayed every day and, for the most part, offered many intentions: Dear God, do this and that, permit this but not that. Contemplation took place in a kind of desolation; apart from 1930, when we were in Wallis and Tessin (in 1929 and 1931 we were in Porquerolles and, in 1933, in Riccione). At that time I was able to contemplate again, somehow walk with God, go for long walks together with him. In 1931, in Porquerolles, I somehow became reconciled: to life, to God, to my fate as a wife, to everything altogether. Of course there was never the least disagreement between Emil and myself; never, never any hard or angry words in these seven years. But I probably did not love him until 1931. Other than as you usually love your fellowmen. I had always watched over him carefully, was concerned about his well-being. But I did not bring an inner enthusiasm to this. We were with Oeri in Porquerolles, and I knew that Oeri was a believer; Emil, however, was then quite far away from faith. On a walk through a pine forest I said to him, "I cannot imagine that God does not exist, and even less that he does not have a special plan for each of his creatures. But everything is so terribly obscured now." In the evening I went for a walk with Oeri along the harbor. All of a sudden he said, "You are interested in the existence of God. I myself believe very firmly; I have a child's faith." Then I realized that Emil had said something to him. From that moment on, the whole situation was eased for me. I understood that my faith was of concern to him. I wept all night long, and afterward the matter was more or less settled. I was terribly tired, had no strength left; the weight of the last four years pressed me down (and on top of it, this was the same day on which Mr. Moulin had drowned). I was in bed, crying. Emil came to my room and sat down next to my bed and simply let me cry. He understood only too well what a sacrifice these four years had been. Once in a while he said a word of thanks or some other little word. From this moment on, I loved him. And even the prayer of earlier days returned. There was once more a *closeness* there, and I no longer needed to resist. Before, a kind of terrible misunderstanding burdened my relationship with God. As if God had given me a bowl of precious liquid to carry and then, again and again, gave this bowl a push so that it lost more and more of its contents ...

Now there was contemplation once again: the sea, the entire landscape, the pines pointing to the sky, the endless water; everything, everything that was so beautiful, now once more became occasion to think of God. I emerged from the past four years as from a tunnel. Everything that impressed me, that gave me pleasure, was again centered in God.

I did not pray much verbally—three or four Our Fathers during the day. And prayer for the patients. I never undertook anything with a patient without having prayed for him. I even baptized children at that time, in 1929, in the hospital for women. From 1931 up until Emil's death in 1934, I prayed; in the end, it was a matter of giving Emil back to God. And then, on a drive home, at a turn near Agno, I knew that now I had to surrender him.

3. *The dark time from 1934 to 1940.* During the two days that Emil was in Clara Hospital, I prayed in the chapel like a madwoman: "Your will be done." And yet I knew that deep down I wanted my will to be done. In my innermost self, I was saying, "God, you can take everything from me, even my practice, which I love so much, only please, not Emil." And then when Emil died and I tried to pray the Our Father, I was terrified. It was as if I were exposed before God as a hypocrite. The two days before Emil's death had been like a desperate defiance; afterward, there was no defiance left at all, rather simply the recognition of my inability to be totally faithful to God; a despair of being able to give consent in full depth. What I completely lacked at that time was the trust that God, in his grace, can compensate for our inability. I simply did not know that. I had much too much the feeling of having to render the entire consent from my own strength.

During all those years I prayed verbally several times every day. But all prayers led back as if automatically to the Our Father, and there it stopped. Moreover, I was intensely concerned intellectually with the question of faith. I was as though possessed by the necessity of getting to the right faith and accepting it. I imagined that the right faith was the Catholic one and if I were in it, my relationship to God would also be right again. Yet, on the other hand, the righting of my relationship to God seemed to me to be the prerequisite for getting there. Herein lay the difficulty, and I kept hoping for an external event that would start things moving. A leap had to be made, and this leap could not be accomplished by intellectual considerations alone. And I also knew that there was a special service, a special mission, and I had to live during these years with the knowledge of the mission but without experiencing it.

Contemplation no longer proceeded so easily and naïvely as before. I had to give myself a push in order to get into it. And the way in which it almost invariably proceeded was that I thought of God, told him of my love and my readiness to serve. I folded my hands and adored him. "I want to be yours, make of me what you will...." And then I again ran into the Our Father. It was no longer as agonizing as in the years between 1927 and 1931, because in those years everything was dominated by the thought that I had made a terrible mistake with the marriage, had upset my whole relationship with God. That was no longer so. Rather, some kind of misunderstanding surrounded this phrase "Your will be done", and some day it would be cleared up.

I talked to Pastor M. about the difficulty once; he thought I should simply pray something different. But, of course, I could not explain my problems to him properly at all. He merely said that one could be entirely Christian without ever praying an Our Father. That was no solution. Another time, I called Pastor von St., asking whether I could speak with him. He said we could surely settle the matter by telephone. Later I went to Pastor H., but he did not even give me a chance to express my question at all. Then afterward I wept terribly in Saint Anthony's Church.

I prayed in Catholic churches in Spain, Italy, and France. There I felt completely at home. When I was in Paris in 1934, after Emil's death, I went to Mass every day. On one occasion, Noldi was confirmed and later Niggi; both times I went to Communion. I cannot remember the first time; the second time, in 1938, I had the feeling that it was absolutely wrong, actually a betrayal.

Even when Emil was still alive, we both seriously considered becoming Catholic. From 1931 on, he believed in God and in redemption. Before that, he had not really believed. We talked a lot to each other about religion. In Italy he went to Mass with me almost daily, and he always prayed with me in the churches. He was completely finished with Protestantism, he said. And what he now believed clearly tended toward Catholicism. We were also friends with the Catholic pastor in Lörrach, Father Haller. When I baptized the first child in 1929, I was uncertain whether I had done it correctly; I spoke at great length with Father Haller then, and Emil was also present. We always had religious conversations when he was visiting us or when we were in Lörrach. Not of a particularly lofty quality, but still....

It was soon after Emil's death that I had my first religious conversation with Werner.[8] He was of the opinion that I was not a believer, and he felt very sorry for me. I somehow explained to him that I was hardly able to pray any more and meant by this that Emil's death had deeply shaken my relationship to God. A few weeks later, I told him that he must have misunderstood me; I did indeed believe in God but did not know where he was. And although I was without a denomination, I believed that I would definitely end in Catholicism. This conversation took place before we were married. He gave me *The Spirit of Catholicism* by Adam to read. In the years 1934–1940, I knew with certainty that this was the only solution. But there was simply no opportunity, and every attempt to talk with a priest failed.

Then, in the spring of 1940, the conversation with Hans Urs. I tell him that I want to become Catholic. He

---

[8] Werner Kaegi, who would become Adrienne's second husband. – ED.

immediately asks me about my prayer. I explain my difficulty with the Our Father; I almost wanted to ask him to pray it together with me. But since he had removed all the obstacles for me, I prayed it that night on my knees at my bedside.

15. ADRIENNE'S RELATIONSHIP TO HUMAN FAULTS

There are people who could almost be regarded as functions of their faults. If you had to characterize them in one sentence, their faults would come to mind first of all. It is the way they present themselves. Then you are startled, realizing that you have failed to approach them in love. Usually where such obvious faults are concerned, it is not at all a matter of grave sins. Thus it is indeed possible to search for a different approach, to construct a different image of this person. And when you have found it, the fault becomes integrated and is no longer nearly as obtrusive as before.

The really frightening sins are usually recognized only slowly by natural sight. They can be revealed to someone suddenly, however, in a supernatural way. And that usually occurs so that you will try to help the person. Many Christians will say, "When I discover such a plank in my brother's eye, I begin first of all with an examination of my own conscience. I try to purify myself, to sanctify myself...." Unfortunately this does not occur to me. I am probably much too careless in this regard. Only when I discover a fault that I do not understand at all do I seek first of all to make it possible in myself, to put myself in the other's place. Not, of course, in such a way that I gradually come to find pleasure in the sin. But I try to imagine the situation from within. Then it always becomes genuinely clear to me. And only then can I talk to the person concerned.

People often lie to you (for example, women who explain to you why they had an abortion), and then you feel a quite definite uneasiness with regard to these "colored" reports. But the extenuating circumstances *I* perceive are really much more extensive, as a rule, than those claimed by the people themselves, even if they originate somewhere else entirely than where these people suspect. In some cases I "see through" completely right from the beginning. But then I often do not know whether this ability to see is founded on a knowledge acquired through experience or whether this perception became spontaneously clear to me like this even earlier.

It can happen that a fault is seen very accurately as a fault and simultaneously comprehended. I prefer to speak of comprehending rather than of excusing, for, after all, I am not a confessor who could remit sins. The lie retains its abominable character, but the liar does not become more alien to me because of his sin. Indeed, I see why he lied, how hard it would have been for him not to lie, how poorly armed he is for this fight for the truth. But I do not, for that reason, say that in his place I would have done it, too. Perhaps this is due, once again, to my carelessness. I really project back to myself only if there is something I do not understand; otherwise, I am out of the picture.

Actually there is only one thing I do not understand: *cruelty*. I can recognize it, to be sure, but I cannot really understand it. It is true that a kind of cruelty against God is involved in any sin. But it is usually not intended as such. What I do not understand is premeditated cruelty. With cruelty, too, there is a kind of projection into myself, but it is unintended; it takes hold of me suddenly, pursues me, does not release me for days.

You reprimand the faults and make them clear to people. But at the same time you love the people and press them to your heart. Or, if I must not be affectionate at the moment because I have to personify authority (for example, in regard to my daughters), I will be affectionate with them afterward in prayer. I can be considerably more gentle with the patients in my practice than with my "children".

You should not reflect the faults of others into yourself, or else you begin to compare and the sin becomes relative. But it should always retain an absolute character. And that "self-knowledge" which a person pursues while taking someone else's sins into himself and observing how easily he, too, could have committed them leads to presumptuousness in the end. You do not attain any objectivity by taking sin into yourself in such a way. It is unhealthy to take every murder, every atrocity into yourself. There is, after all, an outside world; and even if I love my neighbor, he does not therefore have to live in me as Christ lives in me.

"Representative confession" is something completely different.[9] For it is precisely in this experience that I cannot judge anything. Precisely where the confession is personal (I confess for you), I must not begin by first taking your sin into myself in order to "try it on". It is an act without prelude. It would be just as wrong as if—after having been to confession and realizing that I would have to confess again in three weeks—I were to examine myself day by day in order to determine up to what point in time I am still clean and when and how dust gathers and increases until the "measure is full", as it were, after three weeks.

Here the little Thérèse has observed something quite accurately when she says she wants to be a penitent and to be considered as such, that she would like not to have to make a general confession upon entering so that her

---

[9] Cf. *Die Beichte* (1960), 105f. English edition: *Confession*, 2nd ed. (San Francisco, Ignatius Press, 2017), 111 ff.

confessor would not realize that she is not a fallen woman. Such a kind of anonymity is entirely correct; it is truly an authentic form of representative confession. Nor is it disclosed whether she has fallen once or a hundred times. When Francis says he could have committed all sins, even this is entirely Christian with no trace of pharisaism. Only if one begins to analyze this more closely are sins discovered to which he has not the least inclination, which are not at all in the realm of my possibilities. After all, I cannot attribute to myself any male homosexual sin. Or if I hate playing sports, I cannot take the sin of cheating in soccer upon myself as my own. I can take sin upon myself only in its totality—in the totality of sensual sins, in the totality of sins of pride.

When I am in the "gap", it is possible that all perspectives are askew. But there everything will be formed by the Lord, including my view, even my "inclination" toward this or that sin.

16. ADRIENNE AND CONFESSION

I find the Curé d'Ars terribly exciting. He stands exactly at the point where sin and redemption intersect, between the first and the second Adam, between the Cross and the Resurrection. I see him sitting on this point as on a volcano. I think that an SPN—whom I certainly love, God knows—is great: this intelligence, this humility.... But the Curé sits in the very spot where I, too, would like to sit; the only place where I would like to have the office of authority as well. His position is *the* place in the spiritual life. The view from within confession, the *operation* of confession. This full light, which falls precisely between confession and absolution. Every time I confess, I experience it physically as a shock. There are many emotions that one can bear. But to be absolved, even to look forward to this moment, is hardly bearable. Certainly this would be so were it only because of my sins, but these—is one permitted to say this?—do not particularly interest me at all. What is so fantastic is that you can bring other things along ... and that everything that anybody has ever done enters into this bringing-along. ...

When I confess, "I have not loved", I always think I am lying. And not, to be sure, because I have really loved! The lie consists in not being seized at that moment by *my* lack of love—only how shall I express it so that it is true? I really ought to confess that God has not been loved, God has not been adored reverently, my and our neighbor has not received the love that is due him. And what is terrible is that *God* has not been loved, and not that *I* have not loved!

Thus when I confess that I have not loved God enough, this means above all that Adrienne has not seen to it that God is loved. And yet I do not at all know what possibilities Adrienne had for effecting greater love for God, or I know only a few at the most. But what is formidable is that Adrienne is sitting in the midst of a lack of love and is confessing this lack of love at a prescribed moment with any kind of voice appropriate for it, and, moreover, that this confession could be made, at the same moment, with the same words, by a hundred thousand others. And through their confession, all could sense that each believer is sharing the responsibility for all believers. That to confess, as the Lord instituted it on the Cross, is a kind of sign of the Cross over everybody, those who believe and those who do not yet believe. An identification mark that God imprints. And this sign is raised (*relevé*) somewhere by those who come to confession, and by the sign God the Father recognizes the totality: the Cross of the Son, his sacrifice, and also the responsibility of each believer; he recognizes perhaps the love of individuals, but also the lack of love, the opposition, the recalcitrance of innumerable people. And in that, God recognizes "the missing piece". When someone confesses, God can say, "Now I have proof! Now I know that my Son has suffered and why. Now I know that I have created the world and why, and what the truth of the triune God in heaven is!"

When I go to the Curé d'Ars and confess to him, then of course this includes an *opus operatum*. But the astonishing thing is that I go to him and tell him something and he answers that he had expected something entirely different in the name of God, in the name of the Son on the Cross. In the name of the Son forsaken by the Father. And he *knows* the genuineness and truth of my confession and of the whole disposition of my soul. He sees through my untruth, my tepidity and equivocation, and can therefore put his finger immediately on what was hidden by me. And it is this that excites God in heaven himself. It is the enormous excitement of the Lord when he sees the sinful woman coming with the jar of fragrant oil or the woman at Jacob's well, even Nathaniel. Always the moment when sinfulness breaks open and is taken into the light. That is what is explosive in Christianity, and the Curé sits right in the middle of it.

17. ADRIENNE'S DISPOSITION IN CONFESSING
(She is speaking under obedience)

1. *Her surrender in confession.* The most distinguishing characteristic in Adrienne's confessing is that almost invariably her will to surrender is surpassed by God's act of taking. The surrender begins even before the actual confession.

It may arise from herself, when she has the feeling that something is no longer completely fresh and needs purification. Or she may be responding to a demand from God, who wants total confession and surrender. Perhaps what is being demanded is not yet evident. Then an overall surrender is necessary, in any case, as a beginning. But then, during the confession itself, Adrienne frequently experiences that her surrender (in confession) changes into a being-taken by God. Consequently, what she finally says becomes something different from what she had originally planned to say. Metaphorically speaking, you have decided to give an alms from your purse, but God seizes the purse itself. Even while she is preparing for confession, he often does not allow her to choose what she wants to say and how she wants to surrender, rather, he says immediately, "I would prefer such and such."[10] She is responding to a demand that does not correspond to her own expectations. Usually she wished to confess some simple fault that she saw clearly. In the moment of confessing, she no longer sees it. As she kneels down, an entirely different weakness of her soul is exposed. A moment of uneasiness follows. "There was something else I wanted to confess...." And then she sees only her deficient love.

This nakedness in confession points in two directions: to the nakedness of the Lord on the Cross and to that which one has in heaven. But in both directions, this nakedness is removed from one's personal disposal. I cannot now cover myself with a personal confession as with a shirt or a scarf; rather, I am brought into the state of nakedness. But then the penitent is immersed in the slimy reality of universal

[10] Another metaphor: A. says that once, after receiving absolution, she asked me what she was to do for her penance. I was to have answered, "The penance is to do no penance" (which was harder for her than the opposite).

sin. This is inherent in the atmosphere of the sacrament. For that reason, too, I must forgo the attempt to make myself naked: I am covered with slime up to my neck. And when you look at me, you see me covered with all these sins, with which I thought I had nothing in common, at least for the moment. "I am *perhaps* guilty, after all, that one or another of my relatives has not yet become a Catholic or that he has committed a particular sin." But, I think, "After all, I can hardly be blamed for some African chief not having been converted." But it is precisely these gradations that no longer exist in a certain phase of confession. You are confronted with the totality of guilt. I have prayed too little, not given freely enough of my love, so that the Church and the Lord had nothing in reserve. I can never *prove* that it was not precisely *my* prayer that was lacking. Thus my being covered with the slime of sins acquires the character of a different nakedness. I was naked before in disclosing my sins; and more naked still when God uncovered more than I intended to uncover. But now I have to draw something out from this slime, call special attention to it, otherwise my relation to this slime will not be evident. I must expose that part of me which comes in contact with it. And thus, more than ever, I have the feeling that the entire confession stands within the framework of a demand whose dimensions are no longer within my view at all. At first I was prepared to say everything I know, everything within the scope of my vision. But what does "everything" mean, after all? It is an analogous quantity. It can mean everything that I know or can imagine. But it can also mean everything that God wants to hear from me. And this does not make it untrue. Rather, my truth is taken up into the greater truth of God. If God should demand of me that I confess that I am avaricious (which to my knowledge I am not), then I would confess it. And I would do this also for the reason that the concept of ava-rice has at this moment been infinitely expanded and no longer has anything in common with my narrow concept of it. When God looks at avarice, things become evident in it that I had not as yet perceived. And in this nakedness, even I see something of what I had not seen until now. It is as if I had a birthmark somewhere on my body where I could not see. God, however, can undress me and tell me, "There is a spot which you must confess."

It may also happen that you would like to reveal every-thing down to the last detail and the confessor says that it is sufficient to take off the left stocking, and so on. That strikes me as an incomprehensible choice. God can also make such a choice if he wants to. Perhaps in retrospect, one will come to understand why this was right. But it is good if you no longer remain at the helm during confes-sion, no longer know precisely whether you are coming or going. You must learn that you cannot shape everything yourself, that confession is the very place where you are decidedly *being* shaped, and that a reversal of expectations may follow in its wake. And this very reversal can after-ward strike you as what was obviously right.

In confession there is also the point in which you stand along with the crucified Son before the Father. Of course the penitent does not know this and need not imagine it. But, objectively speaking, it is nonetheless true. And now, when the Son bears the sins of the world, he does so, not as *he* sees them, but as the Father, who was offended by them, sees them. And the Son does not claim to know bet-ter than the Father how the Father is affected by sin. The Son's nakedness on the Cross means also for him standing within a truth not cut to his measure.

But confession even goes back to Adam, who, before the fall, lived in a nakedness and a truth that he later lost through sin. In his nakedness, Adam was conformed to truth. But this conformity is missing both in the Son on the Cross and in the sinner in confession. Thus there is the moment in confession when you yourself know nothing more, when you yourself cannot move. Confession resembles a conversation the course of which cannot be predicted.

Nevertheless, preparation is required. Otherwise, God would not, of course, be able to effect a change in you in the course of the confession. And God helps you prepare yourself. He wants the surrender, or the attempted one, for it is the prerequisite for his act of taking you. And in this I must always admit that I have not prepared myself well enough. There is also, however, a certain passive being-prepared that runs parallel to the active preparation.

Confession is an inexhaustible sacrament, one that has many more aspects than we suspect. A lifetime does not suffice to understand it.

2. *Transferring the disposition of confession into everyday life.* The disposition of confession is the attempt, in confessing, to respond to the demand of God. But that is not the end. Through absolution, something new is placed in my hands: an extension of my task; and this consists, above all, in that I continue in the attitude of confession, remain in the same readiness, and that this readiness allow itself to be formed and directed by the priest's exhortation. Let us suppose I am on the road to improvement; seven weeks ago I had seven lies to confess; five weeks ago, five; three weeks ago, three.... If it is progress, this ought to mean that I feel a deeper contrition about today's three lies than about the seven earlier ones. Contrition must increase with a decrease of sin, must ever more take possession of the innermost part of the soul. This can be perceived less clearly during confession itself, but you should be able to

detect it in everyday life. On the one hand, I remember having confessed, but to some extent I also know that I must pass on the grace of confession; and not, of course, as a ready-made grace, but, rather, one within the openness that confession has brought about. In passing on this grace, I must therefore give myself along with it. Since it is a gift of confession, it must be given freely in a disposition brought about by the gift. And I must be ready to remain as open as if I had to confess my sins. But sin, of course, is not the reason why I remain like this; rather, it is indeed confession itself, as gift and experience.

Openness in everyday life is something very delicate. In confession, the confessor acts with authority: he does so in the name of the Church, which thus takes an eminent part in every confession. In everyday life, the Church is much more prominent than the confessor. By receiving the sacrament of the Church, I have assumed, with respect to the Church, a new obligation in my life, mediated by the Church's authority and its exercise. But the priest is not only authority; he is, at the same time, a person. And when the Church is wholly present in the priestly office, this does not take place apart from the priestly person. When the Son exercises the authority of the redeemer on the Cross, he does so with his whole person. And the priest likewise has become confessor for this sinner in the confessional; indeed, he has become priest in order to assume the responsibility for this sinner who is coming to him. As completely authoritative and ecclesiastical as the relationship of confessor and penitent is, it does not for that reason lack a personal side that also has an effect on everyday life after confession. And, of course, in subsequent everyday life the office of authority recedes; it is, as it were, absorbed back into the Church, and the Church is now more prominent as community, in the neighbor.

A confession is never strictly private, although the confessional seal seems to suggest this in the process of confession and absolution. But that is by no means so; precisely so that the secrecy will remain binding, the fruit must belong to everybody. Not primarily through "restitution"—that is only a minor obligation on the periphery, the least that is required, for minimalists. But it will be understood, nevertheless, that this is the least that can be done in view of such an immense grace. Just as a fruit, a pregnancy and birth, must follow the sexual act between husband and wife, which, of course, takes place and remains in secrecy, so an evident fruit must come forth from the secrecy of confession—which will be divulged no more than the secrecy of the sexual act. We would be usurpers if we wanted to live as Catholics without this grace being noticeable in us.

3. *Transference into the heavenly state.* Everyone who is in heaven takes along from his last and definitive confession—last judgment and purgatory—a confessional disposition that remains for eternity. He has attained perfect nakedness and experienced absolution in the fire of judgment. And he can no longer lose the grace of having been definitively judged. In the exigency of his judgment, God worked upon him long and thoroughly until everything lay there open and clear. And the fruit of this process does not remain confined to heaven; there are graces that return to earth from this confessional disposition of the saints in heaven. We sinners do not notice them only because we are not yet in perfect purity. But something of this grace is at work when we on earth take the sins of others upon ourselves in our penance. For this would be too much for a person on earth if he did not have help from heaven. Only the Lord carried his Cross completely alone. Everyone who follows

him in carrying his cross does so within the community of saints in heaven.

18. ADRIENNE AND THE SAINTS

Saints have in each case become important for me after I have seen them. I do not know how I would have come close to them otherwise. The saints played no part at all in the formulation of the whole question of my childhood and youth—that God is different from what the Protestants imagine. Whenever the name of a saint was mentioned, almost invariably it was accompanied by a disparaging remark: "The Catholics do not dare approach God directly. They place human beings between themselves and God, deify them and call them holy and expect things of them that are not at all theirs to give. All of this so as not to have to look at God directly." And I cannot say that I found the objection, which I heard over and over again, especially embarrassing. It did not awaken any questions in me. Only when I possessed the Mother of God— had seen her and adored and loved her and understood her role—did the saints also draw near to me.

I still remember very well how you told me that the Mother of God always has a special part in a conversion; it was then that it also became clear to me for the first time that you had a relationship to the Mother and that one, simply as Catholic, has one. Before, I had seen her more as part of what one must believe as a Catholic, what one "swallows" with the rest without making it a special issue but without having to absorb it into one's innermost being. But when I saw this relationship in you to be a truly living one, the question of the other saints also became acute for me for the first time. But it almost seems to me that the questions about the Mother as well as about the saints became urgent only when the answer was already there: that is, perceived in another person.

The relationship undoubtedly consists in a kind of looking toward with veneration. And I had the impression that certain saints seemed to promote others. The little Thérèse brings me closer, perhaps, to the great one. The little one is clear to me from the beginning. This certainly does not necessarily mean that I should overlook certain of her shortcomings, that she does not exasperate me now and then. But, *enfin*, there is incredible good in her. And this good takes the other that I find less outstanding under its mantle, and in this way it simply passes with the rest. That is true for an individual saint, but it can also take place in the relationship between several saints. One allows me to "swallow" the other. Thus I can tell myself purely intellectually that there would be no Carmel without the great Teresa; she is therefore a prerequisite for the little one; some of the sanctity of the little one has its foundation in the great one.

Neither do I know what my mission is in this: whether it is only my personal impossible character, which does not allow me simply to fall to my knees before the saints, or whether a certain distance and criticism is inherent in my mission. It is often so hard to differentiate between mission and character.

When in my eyes saints truly reflect God's holiness, I am by all means prepared to venerate them. But I feel the same way about some saints as I might, for example, about a great scholar. The fellow who discovered this bacillus impresses me immensely. I am extremely eager to hear the lecture he will give on his discovery. I look forward to it enormously. But for nothing in the world would I personally want to live with him. Maybe he has an unpleasant odor or he does not wash his hands, and so on. This does not prevent me from being impressed by him as a scholar. And perhaps I will put up with his evil-smelling tobacco, and so on, in order to find out more about his bacillus....

With Saint Ignatius, I am somehow so related in my way of thinking that not the slightest misunderstanding occurs. It is perfectly natural for me to converse with him. It is characteristic of him to point constantly toward God. With few saints do I have as strong an impression as I do with him that everything he teaches and discloses always originates in his association with God. In my eyes he is the least pharisaic of all saints. Francis of Assisi, as much as he moves me and as fond as I am of him, does not point to God with the same shrewd intelligence. And at the moment I am intent on intelligence. Ignatius is intelligent by nature. But in a supernatural way, he is even more intelligent because he constantly associates with God and is continuously working with God on the elaboration of his mission. I do not believe, however, that he did very well in school.

I do not want to talk about John. You know well enough what I think of him. I feel a great love for Mary Magdalen because for me she is the embodiment of the working of God's grace. This sinner, who *gives herself away* in sin, wants somehow to give a gift by doing so and then, suddenly and completely, *receives* the gift of forgiveness. I also love the Baptist. This strange groping: he goes and baptizes and fulfills a task before he comprehends his mission. Christ is still to follow him. The Baptist begins without any human certitude. He stakes everything on the one card of the divine, the supernatural.

I also admire Catherine of Siena very much. Her courage simply to write to everyone like that—I would not have dared to do that. And to rebuke the popes in that way. Just think if I were to sit down today and write the pope what I think of him and what he should do differently. And the same with the bishops and other authorities.

And you also know very well that I have a secret passion for the Curé d'Ars. The Church Fathers—I think it was wonderful for them—the entire faith was offered to them in a unity, and they were able to jump into it with their whole being. But now I want to say something impertinent: somehow I feel quite related to these Church Fathers, because you are so totally thrown into the fundamental truths and then must swim therein. This is certainly the case in the mission of all these so-called commentaries: it is really as if you always had to live the fullness of the Gospel you are in the process of describing. Somehow it is something quite primitive: simply to recount what is understood and experienced from within this fullness. Is it not true that others who write commentaries and the like have to study for years, pore over books, collect data, and take into consideration what everybody else has said. For us it means a little bit of love, a little bit of obedience, a droplet of faith, and now go ahead and say how it strikes you. It is amusing. And you have the feeling that the experience is practical; what you say is *experienced* with the spirit or with the body, with faith, with hope, and love. You pay the price with your person. Everything you say is always connected with what has been received directly as a gift and has been experienced; with that for which you are willing to risk your life. It is always personal. Thus the result is a strange mixture of the subjective and objective. Everything you say as answer to a mission under obedience is indeed given to you objectively, but it must, nevertheless, be received and assimilated subjectively. And then suddenly there is a small fruit....

Then also there is Elizabeth of Thuringia, whom I love: first because of her love for the poor, her ability to meet the Lord everywhere in the poor. And also because she does not let herself be repelled by anything, be it ever so repugnant. And then this self-abnegation! I also have the feeling that the priest who directs her does not reach to her toes; but she tolerates it. The treatment he confers upon her makes no difference to her; it does not interest her. In this regard, she reminds me very much of Ignatius. She no longer exists. There is only the Kingdom of God, the glory of God, and she simply proclaims this kingdom as well as she can. She is totally *effacée*. She does not at all take into account that she still exists, that she could lay claim to any special consideration or any mark of honor. And she never looks back; I especially love that in her. She never indulges in self-reflection: for example, how it used to be and how it is now!

Hildegard I love very much, above all for her strength, her imperturbability, her competence. And it is so beautiful the way in which she places what she can do completely in the service of God, and the way in which God in turn grants this human ability a quality of holiness. She does not live two lives, but one. She is the opposite of those people who draw a dividing line between their professional concerns and their piety. She knows what God gives her, but she also gives him all that she can do. And that I think is very, very beautiful. She does not think that God needs complicated prayers and special devotions, or, on the other hand, that her ability is her own personal possession. There is an obvious taking and giving. She does not place any special importance on her own ability. She knows what she is capable of, and that is very natural for her. And God gives it his blessing. And I presume that she continues her professional education as well as she can, but always in connection with the supernatural grace bestowed on her. And it is the same with her as with Ignatius and Elizabeth: she does not consider herself important at all.

Don Bosco is also one who forgets himself in serving. And I also see how, first of all, he wants to help the most impossible people and how, through human need, he gets to know ever better the need of the Lord. "I was naked and you clothed me...." It always seems to be the external, visible need that leads him into the mysteries of the inner need.

Aloysius and Stanislaus are among my favorites. To the end, they preserved purity and a childlikeness in purity. They belong to those saints whom I like to consult, with whom I confer. They have much in common with the "tumbling angels" [*Purzelengeln*].[11] It is said of Aloysius that he could not bear to listen to a coarse allusion. It would be more correct to say that he can subsequently ignore it completely. He leaves what is impure behind and stands with the same natural purity before God and in his mission. Both of them have a certain elasticity; they are like rubber balls that always return to being round. They immediately hand every bad experience over to God and think no more about it. They have the ability to remain the way God wants them; not dwelling on difficulties any longer than is absolutely necessary. They are able to recover their vitality.

Something in Catherine Labouré attracted me greatly. When she heard that the Mother of God was present and that she should go to her, she made no fuss at all about it. For me she belongs to those saints who experienced something once that has a lasting aftereffect, but that does not cause her to consider herself of any significance at all. She has a kind of flair for perfect obedience. And it is most likely not easy for her in her surroundings. It is no more surprising to her that the Mother of God suddenly calls her than if one of the sisters were to tell her to go to

[11] See the *Tagebuch*.

the chapel. The difference from Bernadette lies in the fact
that she already has experience of the convent and knows
several things about mysticism. What is beautiful in her is
that she lets what has to be done happen to her without
wanting to bring it into conformity with her *knowledge*. I
would have liked to have gone to school with these three
in order to share their carefree childhood with them.

19. ADRIENNE, THE SAINTS, AND THE MISSION

In my youth, the saints made no impression on me. Ignatius was present, to be sure, but I do not venture to say
that he made an impression on me as a "saint". Certainly
he awakened a question in me; he pointed me toward
God. Later I thought that the Catholics were fortunate;
for every emergency they have a special saint whom they
can invoke. (Nowadays I myself pray to Anthony when
I have lost something, and when I promise him enough
money for his poor, he always helps me.) But—probably
through Ignatius—it became clear to me even then that
the saints thus invoked always refer you to God. And
I thought at the time: that is a practical system, probably very reasonable. And at some point I asked myself the
question: Should my image of God actually be diminished
by these invocations? Or might it not really be that, on the
contrary, he comes closer to me through the saints, even in
such trifles as those for which Anthony is invoked? At that
time, the question remained open. But I thought that this
was something that must not be forgotten: that there are
saints. I was then around twenty years old. I already knew
at that age that there was a mission that had to be under-
taken for the rechristianization of the world, and perhaps
the saints were necessary here. For me, Ignatius was always

in the background of the question. He was like a clasp that I liked; I thought that one day I would like to wear a dress to match this clasp. If I had happened to come across a book on him in a bookstore, I would certainly have made a dive for it.

(I ask: When did the saints begin to become important to you?) *She:* Are they important at all? I probably love their holiness more than their being saints. I understand quite well that their being holy presents a reflection of God's holiness, an answer to his bestowal of something of his holiness upon us. Certainly, even this answer contains some merit, in my opinion, but I am afraid that for me the moment will come pretty soon when I will say, "You are holy. Very well, but we also have a task, and we cannot spend all our time contemplating your holiness." That is perhaps put a bit crudely, but there is some truth in it. And, moreover, they somehow all belong to the train of the Mother of God.

(I ask: How does one recognize God's holiness in them?) *She:* When you realize how many obstacles exist in a human life and that the saints have conquered them all, then you certainly see how God's holiness shines through them; for example, precisely in this conquest.

(I: Do you prefer your own task to the saints?) *She:* That is a strange question. I do not know how much I like it; I only know that it has to be infinitely important to me. Of course there are days when we would like to give this being-important the name of love. But there are other days when I could almost hate it. Hate is too strong a word, but I often have a "rage". Only I never feel indifferent about it. Often I have the feeling of walking eternally in a circle; you are totally exhausted and have stirred up still more people against yourself, and all because of a task that is not taking shape anywhere, not developing anywhere. Then

you would most like to put the whole thing in a sack and throw it into the fire. No, I cannot say that I always love my task. But what is constant is that it is always important for me beyond anything else. Is it not the presence of God in my life? There are moments when you might think: Why not someone who would do it a thousand times better? But what is that to me, after all? And I would stop at nothing rather than give up my mission. And should I lose it, life would no longer be worth the effort of breathing.

20. ADRIENNE'S INTERIOR DISPOSITION

1. *Standing before God.* When I was little, there was the angel. He turned me very powerfully toward God. I no longer know how long I saw him, but, in any event, even years later—when I had done something foolish or had let myself be trapped into something, had in some way turned from God—I simply *turned myself in,* in a tenth of a second probably told God "I am sorry; I did not mean to forget you; I am glad that you are here."

I want to explain the expression "let myself be trapped": that started with school. Although I liked very much to go to school, it was a great infringement on my interior life because it directed my thoughts along a fixed course. Even in primary school and certainly up to the beginning of high school, I needed the first few seconds of recess in order to find God again. You could then do as you wished during recess itself; it could be filled with your own actions and thoughts. It was not actually prayer, and yet prayer was always in the background. To me recess meant much more *service* than the classes. But often I just let myself be trapped: I was so intensely occupied with classmates or something else that, as a result, I lost sight of the service, "*le sourir au Bon Dieu*". Then there was a moment of return to God. Now, in retrospect, it seems to me as if I had been schooled in this a bit by the angel. It had simply become a habit for me.

Later, when I had such a strong sense in religion classes that everything was wrong, that it had to be different, I forgot about it. Everything became too full of problems for one to be able to find God so quickly. The step was too great. At certain moments, to be sure, there were points of searching for God, of resting in God, a recollected prayer; but in between there was nothing. Certainly, I had a task with respect to my classmates, to my school. But the returning to God, the finding him again, was much less constant. Because God was so different, it just became more difficult to search for him. I was glad when I was able to pray properly two or three times a day: in the morning, perhaps, in the afternoon, and at night.

After Emil's death, the time of prayer became a time of anxiety, of searching, of despair, of the most intense uncertainty, of agony. One would surely like to pray, but one cannot.

1940: Meeting you. New insights into the times of prayer: that it would be possible to live in prayer all the time. And just as the return to God required so little effort in my youth, so now it requires no more effort to be continuously in God. Of course there are special times of prayer: morning meditation, or a few prescribed prayers: the Angelus, the rosary. But these are more like a summary of everything else. When I pray at night with words—this is not always the case; often it takes place without words—the words are something like a summation of the entire day.

2. *The Sacraments.* All my life I longed for the sacrament of confession. And the Protestant Lord's Supper instilled horror in me every time: I realized more and

more strongly that this was not the way. And perhaps my longing for the true Communion did not really grow because I had such a negative attitude toward the Protestant Lord's Supper. I was unable to picture the other sacraments. Baptism was never discussed, and consequently I did not understand anything about it. It was only during the few months of instruction preceding my conversion, when I realized that the problem with the Lord's Supper was settled, that I began to have a *thirst* for Communion, for a union with the Lord. I did know that it was a gift of the Lord; but the realization that it was his *flesh* only dawned on me in the final weeks before my conversion. I knew theoretically that he was "present" in the sacrament, but "flesh and blood", that was entirely new to me. Before I took instructions from you, I was once present at a sermon of yours. What made the greatest impression on me at that time was that you yourself were communicating, that the Lord was within you. From this moment on until confession, Communion became what was most important, what was truly longed for. A few months before entering the Church, I had made a sort of provisional confession; it was then that my longing for the Lord began.

In the conversion itself, baptism, confession, and Communion formed, as it were, a unity at the origin. Together they led me into the atmosphere of the sacraments. From then on, I sensed ever more strongly that heaven is realized on earth through the sacramental disposition, the readiness to receive them. In the sacrament there is always more than we anticipate. That also means that the sacrament has the power to expand the moment of its reception through time and make from time a piece of eternity. At the moment I receive absolution, I am actually outside of time. And thus absolution affects the past and the future.

The absolution of the most recent confession continues to have effect, and the one of the next confession somehow already has an effect beforehand. And I would have to sin quite willfully in order to destroy this twofold effect; I would have to *want* to prove that my sin is more powerful than God's grace and that I can shatter the continuity of his grace.

I am convinced that the "death in Cassina" with the sacrament of the dying that I received at the time and the *farewell to the body* expressed therein has, to a certain degree, given me a new corporeality. Also, a definite experience of the conjugal sphere, which I was to describe under obedience, would not have been possible without the last sacraments.

The sacraments are like a net, like a space within which God's call remains alive. And, when it might become a bit tedious for us to be still in the world, the world of the sacraments gives us a strength that comes as an anticipation from heaven.

3. *Penance.* It can belong to prayer, to meditation. And often, when you have been indulging in some earthly pleasure—a good dinner, a friendly conversation, a concert, and so on—you are glad to return to God's atmosphere, and penance brings about the transition. You are more quickly completely detached again. Temptation constantly invites you anew "to enjoy yourself". For example, when you have been at a party where everything was very elegant, the conversation of high quality, and so on, you would like to remain in such an atmosphere; you do not want to surrender it again immediately. At such a moment, penance becomes something quite natural, necessary, even when you are not conscious of being unfaithful toward God.

There is another reason for penance: in order to take part in something. It is the same as with prayer: I begin to pray with a certain intention, and then it simply passes over into the Lord's intentions. And if the limit of penance has not been fixed precisely by obedience, the moment almost invariably comes in which the Lord's suffering appears so much beyond measure that your personal penance seems of no consequence and you carry things to excess.

Or there is penance without any particular intention: you do not begin with something definite; rather, you try right away to throw something into the Lord's sack and to do penance anonymously, without wanting to specify the intention. Generally speaking, I always have the feeling that one does penance anonymously, even when the intention is specified: you are simply *someone* doing penance along with so many others. Precisely who is doing it is totally unimportant.

PART III

ADRIENNE VON SPEYR— PRAYERS

I

PRAYERS OF THE EARTH

1. MORNING PRAYER

Father in heaven, you divided the day from the night so that both might become a reminder and a joy for us: a reminder for us to think of you; a joy in serving you in every way. And so this day which is now breaking should also belong to you. It should become a day of your Church, a day of your children. It is still quite fresh, and it is as though anything could still be formed out of it. And we know that it is your possession, for you have created it, and that in obedience to you we should make of it a chosen day, a space in which you can be at home at every moment and everywhere, a space that is filled by you, but in which you also demand of us that we serve the mission you point out to us. Help us to be pure, give us a good disposition, help us to do joyfully what our service requires.

You divided the day from the night, but grant that we do not constantly divide what we like to do from what appears troublesome to us. Rather, help us thankfully and gladly to accept as coming from your hand everything the day brings us. Help us to cooperate in it interiorly, to make of it what you have ordained. Help us to be as keen of hearing as the day is clear and transparent to you. And when the day brings cloudiness and obscurity, we know that it is the obscurity of our unstable nature, of our ignorance, that makes decisions difficult.

You not only divided; you decided from time immemorial: help us to enter into our task with determination and to decide in the way that you expect. Out of love, you divided day from night; let us live on your love, let it take effect in us, let us offer up each daily task along with your Son, so that it may be fulfilled in your Spirit. Amen.

2. PRAYER AT THE BEGINNING OF MASS

We have come together, Lord, in your house. Help us to recognize not only in the outer signs that we are in your dwelling. Please help us even more to feel your Spirit, so much so that we kneel down before you already changed, ready to accept everything that you would show us, ready also to leave behind us everything that is incompatible with you. And, just as we close the door behind us when we enter your inner room, so let us forget what belongs only to this world, what tends to keep our thoughts away from you, everything that does not belong to your love and is incapable of serving it. You see very well how weak and imperfect we are, with what effort we made the decision to come to you today, how momentous we consider every obstacle, how eager we are to walk ways other than yours. Take away from us, Lord, this wicked heart. Help us to foster pure thoughts; let us become aware in spirit that we are with you, that we await you, that not only your presence before us but your indwelling within us is promised and bestowed by you. Bless this hour. But bless it not only for us, but for all who are with us here. For the priest who is celebrating, for all priests who are celebrating Mass today all over the world, and also for those who are prevented from celebrating. Bless it for all believers, for the whole communion of saints. Bless it also for all those who are on their way to you, who have not yet received the gift of faith, for those who perhaps wait with burning desire to be allowed to step before you at last. Bless it in our lands, bless it in the missions, bless it everywhere where people are and bless it in such a way that they will bear fruit: that we will all stand before you detached from ourselves, so as to see only you. That we will at last follow the path away from ourselves, toward you. That during this hour we will not think of everything possible that has nothing to do with you, but rather that we will pray for that to which you direct us, with an open spirit, because you open your Spirit to us; with a humble heart, because you want to dwell in such hearts; with a loving soul, because you are love itself. Bless us, open us, bestow on us your love. Amen.

3. PRAYER BEFORE THE SERMON

When you preached on earth, O Lord, you found divine words that had the power to reach the hearts of your listeners. Your truth penetrated them and caused them to follow and to live for you. Lord, now bless, too, the words of the preacher. Grant that he may forget himself, his mediocrity, the success that he would like to achieve, in order to be able to speak only and truly of you and your teaching; to say the things awaited by all who listen— something that really comes from you, that is charged with your love, filled with your wisdom, which is not the wisdom of this world. Grant, Lord, that he may be permeated by the Holy Spirit and that he may become a true mediator of your Word. But also grant to us who listen a keen mind so that we really perceive your Word and do not, in our faultfinding, merely become annoyed by the mediocrity of what is said, by the imperfect manner of expression, eventually seeing only the preacher and his weakness and nothing more of your Word and Spirit. Rather, let this hour become a sacred hour where the mediator and the listener are united in your Spirit. Grant that we accept your Word as the living Word of God and allow it to become effective in us, that we take it home with us afterward, so that a bit of the Church may come into being where we are, so that our week may be filled with what your grace bestows on us today. Do not let us forget what we have heard, but help us to develop it. Give us the love that is needed for such a development; let it work in us. Continue to be the light of our days, become the goal of our love, and through this sermon, bestow on us a new life of our faith, a life that may be at once prayer and work in your love. Amen.

4. PRAYER AFTER COMMUNION

Father, you have given us your living Son, and you allow him to come to us over and over again in the Host. You do not give him to us as just any life, but as life from your life. Help us to receive him in all his divine power, which he possesses by means of his surrender. Let us so withdraw before him that he can work in your Spirit, that he can feel at home in us despite all our imperfections and weaknesses, that he can bring forth what you want from our hearts and nothing will be thwarted or diminished by us. Do not allow us to set limits, to know cautions and fears that are foreign to him. Help us to emulate and, insofar as we are able, to follow him. You grant the grace to receive him to so many today; grant that each of them takes along the others who are prevented or not permitted or who do not know him in such a way that they feel a complete long-ing for him. We thank you, Father, that you let the Son become man, that you permitted him to make the sacrifice of the Cross and also granted him the sacrifice of the altar. We thank you for all the grace that every one of us expe-riences through him. But preserve in us the thirst for these graces. Grant that we may always ask for them, not only for ourselves, but for all men, for whose sake your Son died on the Cross and who together with him and through him will rise again by the power of the triune God. Father, bless every Communion, let the meaning of the Eucharist be ever more alive in your Church, and grant that this vitality not be bound by the limits of our recognition and desire, but let it flow forth unhindered from its source: the eternal life. In our thanksgiving, we are united with all those who know you and are privileged to experience the blessings of your Son's mission. And also with all those who endeavor to consecrate their lives to you as proof of their gratitude. Give us the power to fashion this gratitude in such a way that you see in it the working of your Son, that you recognize in the spirit of our thanksgiving your Holy Spirit and can use us for what you will. May we be willing through the willingness of your Son, be loving through the love with which he carried out his mission: to love you in perfect obedience; and thereby deliver us unto you. Amen.

5. EVENING PRAYER

All of your faithful, Lord, see how night is falling; they have done their day's work, grant them rest. A rest that comes from you, that accompanies them, takes from them the burden of the day and the cares and anxiety, and lets them become completely refreshed. Give them good thoughts and fruitful prayer. Let them sense your nearness; let them feel your goodness. Let them fall asleep with you in their thoughts. And when they awaken again, they shall know that you were with them and will not forsake them but help them and will order all things anew for the day ahead. For you can give them new strength, let them see things differently, begin anew. Be with those who sleep and with those who cannot sleep. And if they cannot sleep because they are tormented by worries, lighten these for them. And if they cannot sleep because of pain, show them the meaning with which you yourself have invested suffering so that they feel your presence through the pains that they must suffer now. Give them fruitful thoughts with which they can accompany even the worst agonies. Receive in grace whoever dies this night; bring him to the Father as your brother; give him your forgetting of his sins; give him a new life that lasts forever. And be with your Church. Be in all these dark churches which are deserted at night, in which you alone keep vigil with your small, eternal light. Fill the space completely with your presence so that those who enter early tomorrow morning will receive the gift of a new power of prayer. Be with your whole Church, who is your Bride: help her to live as befits a bride, not led astray by any temptation. Above all, bestow on her that love which united you and your Mother, that love out of which the Mother became a bride to you, just as today your whole holy Church should be your Bride. Sanctify all of your Father's creation; live in everything that your Father has created as a sign that his work is good, as a confirmation of redemption. And let the Holy Spirit blow through the world so that it might be converted and that you might return to the Father his redeemed creation made perfect. Amen.

6. BEFORE THE TABERNACLE

Lord, I want to thank you for your presence, for recognizing in this house the house of your Father and for dwelling within it, so as not to be distant and hidden from us with the Father and the Spirit but, rather, to remain among us as the way that leads to the Father, as the way by which we will also attain the possession of the Holy Spirit. I want to thank you for being here, veiled in the mystery of the Host, but so fully present that you yourself teach us to pray and help us to live. You are so fully present that we come to receive from you and take with us what your presence bestows upon us: the certainty of faith, the love of your dwelling among us. Lord, you know how weak and distracted we are and how we consider everything else more important than you; but again and again you guide us back to this place where you dwell in order to change us. Lord, let your Spirit at last take possession of us so that on all our ways we sense your company, know of your help, your answer; you who do not ask to be adored like a foreign prince but are our brother, our lover who accompanies us always. Help us to live for this love which unites you with the Father in the Holy Spirit. Help us to perceive or divine it everywhere, so that we may be, no longer an obstacle for his working, but channels for your grace. Channels to such an extent that with your help we may stand in your service, cooperate in your work, bring to you new love-filled ones in order to increase that love in the world which desires to encounter you, the Father, and the Spirit. Your presence here is the presence of your love to us. It is wholly an act of love, which also includes within itself every state, every disposition of love.

When you became man and dwelt among us as a child, your Mother stood beside you and gave you the purest love; but even this love was a gift of your presence, given to her by you. It was mother-love that smoothed your path, served you, knew nothing but concern for you in the adoration of the Father in the Son. You formed this mother-love so that it would also be an example to us. Teach us to look at your Mother, help us to love you with her love, let us, together with her, adore you and please you in the same service of love. Amen.

7. PRAYER TO THE RISEN CHRIST

Lord, we thank you for the feast of Easter. We thank you for having returned to us after your death and descent to hell, after you had endured all forsakenness, for having remembered our small forsakenness and for having overcome it by the fullness of your presence. Although you suffered death, for which we are guilty because of the weight of our sins, you return to us as our brother with the gift of your redemption. You do not make us suffer for bringing you to the Cross; rather, you let us share in your joy. You celebrate a reunion with us as if we had never been unfaithful, as if we had been waiting for you continually with faith and confidence, as if we were capable of adding something ourselves to your joy. We are those redeemed by you, and yet you remain our brother. Lord, help us to be thankful. Let the gratitude we owe you and your Mother always accompany us from now on; let it become fruitful and perceptible everywhere in our service. Let us be people redeemed who really fill their whole life with your redemption, who accompany you everywhere, who seek to do your will, as you do the will of the Father. Let us not only enjoy the fruit of your suffering and redemption, but rather help us—beginning today—in our attempt to know you as our brother, our true redeemer forevermore in our midst. Help us never to forget that you are there, that you have answered our unfaithfulness with faithfulness, our disbelief with ever greater grace. Let every day, whether hard or easy, become one that includes the explicit, or at least the hidden, joy of knowing that you have redeemed us and that, in returning to the Father, you take us along. We ask you for your Easter blessing in which the blessing of the Father and the Spirit are contained. Amen.

8. PRAYER FOR THE RENEWAL OF THE SPIRIT

Dear Lord, you see how we become used to everything. Once, we gladly took up your service with the firm intent of being wholly surrendered to you. But, since every day brings nearly the same thing over and over again, it seems to us that our prayer has been circumscribed. We limit it to ourselves and to what seems necessary for just the task at hand so that in the end our spirit has assumed the size of this small task. We ask you not to allow us to narrow ourselves in this way; expand us again; bestow on us again some of the power of Mary's assent, which awaits in readiness the entire divine will, which is always as all-embracing as when it was first pronounced and which is daily confirmed anew. She may have been glad or afraid or hopeful, weary of the daily work or led to the Cross: always she stood before you as at the first, obeying everything you said, hoping to do everything you wished. Behind every one of your wishes, even the smallest, she saw the great unlimited will of the Father that you, the Son, were fulfilling.

Grant that we contemplate and affirm you and your Church, carry out what our mission demands, in an ever new spirit, in the spirit of the Mother's assent. Grant also that we pray for this spirit. We know you yourself are where you send your Spirit. The Spirit brought you to your Mother; the Spirit enabled her to carry you, to give birth to you, to care for you; and because in her you found again your own Spirit, from her you formed your Church. And, since you have called us into this Church, make from each one of us a place where the Spirit of your Church blows, where the will of your Father, our Father, is done together with you and with the help of the Holy Spirit so that we may dare to pray together with you in all serious-ness: Our Father, who art in heaven.... Amen.

9. PRAYER FOR INDIFFERENCE

Lord, you know that I want to serve you but am always still hanging on to my work and opinion; that again and again I hastily crawl back into myself in order to consider everything from my point of view: that I do this, in order to avoid that, wish this, and abhor that. But, in your whole life on earth and especially on the Cross, you have shown us what it means to do the will of another. For you, this other person was the Father, a Father so perfect that, from the beginning and without forming your own opinion, you considered and accepted each of his decisions as per-fect. You did this, not through an insight that would have been the result each time of examination and deliberation, but out of love. Your love for the Father has once and for all taken the place of every personal examination. And this love you also bestowed on your saints; and your holy Ignatius has spoken and written about it. He has demon-strated how decisive the will of the superior, the will of the Father, the divine will itself is for the one who loves and no longer wants to know anything except the desire of the beloved. Give us of your filial strength; grant that we learn to love the Father as you love him. Grant that we reach him through you and your attitude, that we become obedient by your perfect obedience, indifferent through your indifference. Grant that we no longer seek our own will in anything, but that we go directly to you, together with your holy Ignatius, and become indifferent down to the bottom of our hearts, not so as to become indifferent to you and the world, but to begin finally to love you and the Father in the Holy Spirit more than anything else. Amen.

10. PRAYER OF THANKSGIVING AFTER CONFESSION AT THE END OF THE YEAR[1]

Lord, we thank you for having given confession to us, for having taken all our sins away by your death. You have thereby shown us how perfect nakedness before the Father, standing in readiness before him, doing his will, remaining where he has placed us, belongs to true confession. And now that we stand at the end of this year, we recognize that we have often failed. We have left undone much that, according to your will, we should have started. We have not sufficiently obeyed your voice, have not really lived for you alone. For we should really have sought you in all things, should also have delighted in the joys as having come from you, should have taken the sufferings upon ourselves as willed or permitted by you, should have walked each path you opened to us. And yet we need not look back with sadness on this year because, like all years, it was a year of your grace. A year in which you have helped us, encouraged us time and again, made us gifts of joy and a multitude of blessings beyond counting. And while we have not recognized you everywhere, and so often have not lived up to your expectation, today, through your grace, we can have the debris removed from us. You purify,

[1] New Year's Eve, 1951.

you clear away, in us and together with us you accomplish something new. And all of this through the power of your Cross. You suffered this Cross on Good Friday, and despite our failure you let this be followed—in virtue of your Resurrection—by so many feasts of the redemption. And the absolution you give us is a perfect one: with the Father in your Holy Spirit, in your triune, eternal purity, you give back to us a new purity. And thus we need not continue to build on what was imperfect and weak, but we may begin anew on the foundation of your own perfection, which you impart. We may become part of your edifice, go with you, hope with you, work with you. Thus confession radiates into our everyday life; thus absolution takes effect. It radiates and effects the joy whose origin lay in your Cross and which was sufficient to show us your mission every day of the past year. So we thank you for having done everything as befitted us. We thank the Father who let you become man for our sake; we thank your Holy Spirit who constantly endeavored to carry out your mission in our lives. Amen.

11. PRAYER IN THE REALM OF TIME[2]

Father, you have entrusted us with fleeting time as a gift of your grace and presence. Just as you live in eternal time, we must be in transitory time as long as we live; not abandoned by you, but in a relation with you that you have destined and freely given from creation, one that has acquired a new density and capacity through the advent of your Son. And if the years melt away, they are, after all, only days strung together, passing through us as we pass through them in order to seek constantly what you show us, to experience constantly your love anew, to remain

[2] The following prayers were written for a sick woman religious.

constantly embraced by you as all of time continues to
be embraced by your eternity. We know that we are in
your hand, that you order everything. We know that you
demand from us only one thing: the attempt to love you
as steadfastly as we can, not you in isolation, but you with
your Son and your Spirit in that unity you display from
the very beginning of eternity. Our love can be nothing
but an answer, love returned, because you—triune, eternal
love—always love us first. But do not allow this answer to
slacken in us; rather let it be so strong that you can continually perceive in it the reflection of your light. Amen.

12. THROUGH MARY TO CHRIST

I

Through you, Mother, we have come to your Son. You
conceived him; you carried him; you gave birth to him.
You accompanied him all his life in order to bring him
and give him to us, to show us, too, how a human being
can bear him and understand him, how a human being can
place his life within the life of your Son, in order to
receive it from him. In order to convey to us the gift of
his childhood years, his years with you, the gift of his years
in public and the time of his suffering. You were present
everywhere in such a way that all that conveyed his presence was absorbed by you, Mother, yet not for yourself,
but for us. By your consent, you placed yourself at the
disposition of the Father, the Son, and the Holy Spirit in
such a way that the triune God gave us to the Son through
you. You led us to him, but you were always so much in
God, so much within your mission and your own assent
that you wanted to appear everywhere only as mediatrix
and not as giver. But precisely in this way, the mediation
also became a gift that sprang from your humility and that

your humility bestowed on us—a gift to us, but also a gift to God. And today we would ask you to receive anew into your assent everything that makes up life—the joys, but also the sacrifices, the ways that we follow and that we had not foreseen—so that through you we may reach the Son anew. And, through you who knew so well how to accomplish the Son's will, may we ourselves accept anew, desire anew what he has destined for us in the Father's will, because it is his will. But may we also desire anew through you, together with you, in thankfulness that everything done by you took place entirely in obedience to him. And when the sacrifice costs more than we thought, when it is harder to bear, then we want to remember that you did not shrink back from any sacrifice and you did everything in the joy of the assent. And we want to ask you to intercede for us with the Father, with the Son, and with the Spirit so that we might live from your strength, truly reaching the Son through you, and that we might do in him what you have done for him from the beginning.

And when you see your angel, Mother, remember that his appearance gave you assurance of the way. Ask him, out of love for you, to care for us, too, as he cared for you, to intercede for us as he interceded for you and, in his appearance, gave you the strength to consent to everything in faith.

II

Lord, before you became man and entered into suffering, you invited your Mother to serve you as a mother, to suffer your sacrifice with you, but also to share your joys with you. And the grace you granted her and by which she became your Mother is so inexhaustibly great that there is room in it for all who search for you, for all those who would like to offer sacrifice to you in faith: the sacrifice of a life in your service, perhaps also the sacrifice of giving up this service or the sacrifice of unforeseen humiliations and sufferings. And since you loved your Mother so much and bestowed on her such a pure love for you, we ask you, Lord, to take us into this grace daily. In your relationship to your Mother, we ask you to allot us a place that would allow us to offer up to you each of her sacrifices anew, to experience each of her joys along with you, and to do precisely and forever that which the Mother, together with you, the Father, and the Spirit and all the heavenly host, expect of us. Give us the joy and the grace of service now and in eternity. Amen.

13. PRAYER FOR THE RIGHT USE OF SICKNESS

Lord, bless those who are sick; all those who know or feel that they are sick, all those who are in pain, all those who must soon die. Do not bless them merely so that they are able to endure; bless them also so that they learn to endure for you and to see a grace in suffering. Show them that every suffering has received a meaning through your suffering on the Cross, a meaning that is taken by the Father into the meaning of your own suffering and is used for the redemption of the world. Show them that pain and sickness become fruitful if they are willing to suffer in your name, that you can use them to help others, to ease the burden of others, to make passable roads that otherwise could not be traveled. Give them not only strength and courage; give them patience. Finally, give them love for the sufferings that are demanded of them, that love which can only spring from your love and which only together with your love can bear fruit, even if these fruits remain hidden from their view, even if they do not know exactly where you want to use the grace that springs from their suffering. Through your grace, grant that in their sickness they may radiate such love that it may have a contagious effect on others, that their suffering, perhaps, in a hospital ward, may serve to transfigure the suffering of the others, show the nurses and physicians who are dealing with them something they did not know before, disclose the meaning of life and death in a new way to the visitors who come to them. Grant all of them such growth in you that in the end they accept everything gratefully as coming from your hand and that they see in every pain something that surpasses all pain: your grace. Amen.

14. PRAYER FOR THE TIME OF FATIGUE

Dear God, I am too tired to pray. And you certainly know from the Cross how great fatigue can be. I ask you to let all your angels and saints so adore you that no break in adoration results. Amen.

15. PRAYER OF AN ELDERLY WOMAN RELIGIOUS

Dear God, you know that I became a religious in order to serve you and that the decision to do so was not all that easy. You gave me confidence then; I knew that you had chosen this way for me yourself, and every day, all my life, you have given me anew the courage to attempt to sacrifice everything for you. But you know very well the way it is with a life that should be dedicated to you: small and greater sacrifices recur with a kind of regularity, and we get a little used to it. And now you demand a very great sacrifice of me: religious life as you gave it to me I must again give back into your hands. I can no longer walk, can no longer work, can no longer choose for myself what I can sacrifice to you during the day. Sacrifice has taken on a different form now: I must simply accept everything and can only offer you always anew the desire that everything may take place according to your will. Please show me how I can do it so that you are satisfied, so that you recognize your service in me, so that I no longer carry it out, but you in me—you together with your Mother and all the saints—so that this work may be fruitful and may share in the fruitfulness of every hour of your life. I ask you to help me also in my weariness so that I may not tire of sacrificing everything to you. And bless this suffering for your whole Church and for all who seek the way to you. Amen.

16. PRAYER AS DEATH DRAWS NEAR

Lord, because we do not take your death seriously enough, and therefore rarely think of it, the thought of our own dying also remains alien and removed. Even when grave harbingers warn us, we know how to suppress the thought of our death and to continue living as if our earthly existence were unending. And then one day we realize after all that we must die; Lord; grant that we be not completely unprepared then. Help us to see our death in connection with your dying, that is, to know that you died for all of us and that when we die, we can no longer help but be together with you. The punishment that was our death, you have transposed and transformed into the grace of the future eternal life. We can rejoice in this gift of yours. Even when the passage is difficult, even when pains increase, anxiety mounts, and uncertainty overpowers us: all of this agony is to take place, if it is your will, so that you might receive something from our life, a late fruit, which finally stands at your disposition. Help us to die according to your will, perhaps in fear, perhaps in absolute pain, perhaps in our sleep, or experiencing death drawing near hour by hour, but in any case in such a way that we do not forsake the thought of you, but know that every death, even the dark one, is your possession and has died in you on the Cross. Help us to die as believers, that our faith may also shine upon the others present at our dying, that it may be of help to them and later, perhaps, also be of comfort to them when their own hour comes. Lord, make your presence known to all who are left behind; help them to overcome their grief; be with them to the end of their days. Amen.

17. THE *SUSCIPE* OF SAINT IGNATIUS

Take, Lord, and receive. Take my whole life; take it, I ask you, just as it is now, with all that it is, with my strengths, my intentions and efforts, but also with everything that still pulls away from you, that I have set aside for myself; take all of that, too, together with the rest that I offer you. Take everything that all may be yours.

All my liberty. The liberty of my days, the liberty of my thoughts, the liberty of my work, even the liberty of my prayer. From all this liberty, fashion a pure service of your own liberty; dispose freely of mine, therefore, see in it nothing except my desire to serve you. That is the choice that I now make as I leave all my liberty to you.

My memory, my understanding, and my entire will. Take my memory that it may no longer be filled with things that belong to me, but may be emptied and at your disposal in a new way, in order to receive only what you put into it. Take it as an object that until today served a particular purpose and has now become available for any kind of use you have in mind. And take my understanding, which clung to so much, sought to comprehend so much that was not of you; let it become an understanding of your service, at your disposal, that it may take in only that by which you want to enrich it and with which you can do something. Therefore, let everything that is incompatible with you and your intentions sink from sight. Take also my will, which was often only self-will, which time and again withdrew from your will. Take it away from me at last and fashion from it something like a particle of your will that is always fulfilled in doing the will of the Father.

All that I have and possess, thou hast given all to me. You have given me the things that I need for living, my daily food, life with all its small, often superfluous comforts. You have also given me time from your own store of time, days for working, nights for resting. You have given me thoughts and prayer and ultimately everything that I myself am and have and will become. All this is your gift, and I have no right to anything. I did not earn any of it myself and did not receive anything from anyone else but you.

To thee, O Lord, I return it. Not because I scorned and rejected it, for I want to offer it to you just as I received it, as little damaged as possible, with no other meaning and value than the one you intended when you gave it to me. I would also like to offer it to you as fully alive as I received it from you.

All is thine, dispose of it wholly according to thy will. May it be entrusted to you in such a way that you can use it without having to consider or spare the giver, like something you can use or not as you please; I beg you, regard it as your possession as, I am sorry to say, I looked on it as my possession while it was in my hands. I would like to give it to you without calculation or reservation and henceforth in everything, in things and days and nights, see only that which belongs to you, is at your disposal, and is already in that way receiving a new meaning.

Give me thy love and thy grace. Your love was always the triune, divine love in which you gave us a share and which we forfeited through our sins. This time give it to me in such a way that I will esteem it as the highest good and show myself to be not always entirely unworthy of it. I need it more urgently than the air I breathe; let me need it so urgently that it becomes a stimulus to serve you better. It, too, shall be offered to you with everything else; grant that I may treasure it even as you yourself love the Father whom you obey.

For I am rich enough. Rich and capable of serving you, for in your love is contained everything needed by one who believes and hopes. I am as rich through this love as you yourself were in your return to the Father after having fulfilled your mission. As rich as the Father when he received you, as rich as the Spirit when he brought you both together, because your triune love is so infinite that there is room for all in it and so enriching that a creature who lives on the love and grace of God can be filled to overflowing with goods. For faith can desire nothing more ardently than to share in eternal love, and love in eternity can only love itself in its triune fulfillment. Amen.

18. PRAYER THAT SAINT IGNATIUS TAUGHT ADRIENNE

Corpus Christi, adoro te tribus sub tuis formis,
  sub forma divina, simili deo patri,
  sub forma hominis, sacrificii et crucis,
  sub forma hostiae rotundae, sine principio et fine.

Ubi es, est amor sempiternus,
  omnia tangens quae creavit pater,
  omnia quae passus est filius,
  omnia quae vivificat spiritus.
Amorem tui cum gratia mihi dones, ac dives sum satis nec
  quidquam ultra posco. Amen.

Body of Christ, I adore you under your three
      forms,
    under the divine form, in which you are like
      the Father,
    under the form of man, of sacrifice, and Cross,
    under the form of the Host, round, without
      beginning or end.
Wherever you are is eternal love, touching
    all that the Father has created,
    all that the Son has suffered,
    all that the Spirit quickens.
Give me your love and grace, then I am rich
      enough and
    desire nothing more. Amen.

19. PRAYER FOR CONSTANCY

Lord, our God, give your children perseverance in their
love toward you. You know all too well how we are:
moved by your goodness when it comes to us unexpect-
edly, taken aback by your severity when it is revealed in a
demanding way. In experiencing the joyous and the difficult days, we think of you, realizing what comes from you.
But in the monotony of everyday life, we become lukewarm, we forget you; we keep you far from our thoughts
and our work. It is as if we only needed you on eventful
days, as if we wanted to have you at our command. We ask

you to change this; let us turn back while there is still time; you command, uproot our lukewarmness, replace it with fire or cold or with both at once. But allow your Spirit to blow in us. Destroy everything that is not of you and help us to form no ideas of which you are not the center, so that we are thus compelled to a more living love. We do not ask that this love be full of pain or full of bliss, only that it be yours, forever and ever.

Lord, give us the grace to offer you over and over again what you gave us; only in this way will we, unprofitable servants, not remain unfruitful.

Bless your love in us that it may bear the fruit that you desire. Amen.

20. PRAYER FOR THOSE WHO HAVE TURNED AWAY FROM YOU

We can understand death and sickness and even distress, Lord, but that someone can turn away from you after having known your grace remains unfathomable to us. It would, after all, be easy for you to make the signs of your grace so obvious that they could no longer be doubted, or, with a gentle call, fetch back those who are turning away; and you do not do so, do not do so in your wisdom. Lord, let us nevertheless ask you for this with all our heart: grant that our cry penetrate the indifference of those who are withdrawing, allow our members to suffer for them, accept every sacrifice for them; but—we implore you— make their return possible, make it easier, and let us pay whatever price you think fitting for this. We will strive to give you what you will accept, but bestow on them anew your faith, your grace.

And yet we know that again and again we, too, take our faith too lightly, are easily inclined to promises that seem too difficult to us when it comes time to keep them. Lord, give all of us your mercy, and strengthen our weakness.

21. PRAYER FOR DELIVERANCE FROM SELF

Lord, deliver me, and take me to yourself. You have shown me the fetters that hold me back on my way, and if they are still a hindrance, it is most likely because in my innermost being I am not yet willing to separate myself from them. How often do I sigh and regret having so little freedom, yet I am only thinking of the bonds that come with my daily life and profession. But these bonds do not really obstruct the path, they do not influence its actual course, or at most only its exterior form; perhaps on the whole they are only minor trials. What weighs heavily does not come from outside; it lives and is formed in my own self; it is all that I am attached to, all that I do not want to do without, that serves as support and consolation, all that I believe myself entitled to. Take, Lord—I am trying to ask this earnestly of you—everything that in my eyes belongs to the legitimate possession of my soul but that paralyzes my love for you, that makes your love for my neighbor come to a standstill and freeze within me. Grant that I may disappear in the flow of your love to all men, so that it may pour forth unimpeded. Amen.

22. PRAYER FOR USEFULNESS

Father, let our whole life become a prayer that rises up to you like a fire. In its flame may it sweep along everything that is bad and impure, that which is our own and that which is alien, so that you may fill it with your spirit. Let it become so good that it becomes yours and can be used by you. Lord, do not forsake what is evil in us, either, but change it; help us to become open to your actions, even to the painful ones. Grant us conversion; grant it in your own name. Amen.

23. IN THE PASSION

Lord, in your Passion your glory disappears more and more; as the Son of Man, you become mere man, so infinitely like us in your misery and nakedness. And when we contemplate this, as often as you truly grant this to us, we remain before it as if in timelessness. And what we experience is frightening in its duration, but even more frightening in its content. Everything in us turns into being-only-man, that is to say, into loneliness; more: into forsakenness. So much did you suffer for us in the night that even we no longer know that there is a Resurrection. Lord, the weight of our sins on your shoulders becomes unbearable for us. Mark the way, give it the form that you want, that of a cross if it must be. Amen.

24. SURRENDER OF WHAT I DO NOT OWN

Lord, so often I gave you what I possessed in abundance; let me now offer you everything that I do not have, what until now has been denied me, what I have sought, suspecting that it might be unattainable: tranquility, rest, security. And now when I know that it belongs to you, remains in your safe-keeping, your possession, then I will no longer call for it. The idling of my restlessness no longer troubles me: in you is tranquility; you have taken possession of it, even from me; you can redistribute it without loss; in you is security—who else would have it otherwise—you can bestow it. Praise be to you, what we are seeking is found in you, and what we imagined ourselves to be giving voluntarily was in you from the beginning. And yet we thank you for accepting it from us nevertheless. Lord, do not only take what we do not have: keep it.

Only the Lord can plant, to us perhaps he leaves the gathering of a few ears of his corn that have sprouted; we offer him what was already his. A living fire does not stop burning until everything has been consumed and turned to ashes; no one, however, pays attention to the ashes. Scattered on the earth, lifeless, hidden as they are, they cannot fertilize, but they can still be ground completely into the earth, serving a function of which they know nothing. Lord, burn us to ashes and scatter us according to your will. Should I ever still say what I want, do not grant it; even against all appearances, believe that I am yours alone and know no other will but yours. Amen.

II

THE PRAYERS OF HEAVEN[1]

1. "THE GLORY OF GOD GAVE IT LIGHT, AND ITS LAMP WAS THE LAMB"

Lord of omnipotence and Lord of impotence, you reveal everything simultaneously in your holiness: your omnipotence, which has the power to conquer and lead each one of us, and your impotence, which is dependent on the love and surrender of each one of us. You place all your holiness, as the light in which he can walk, at the disposal of each one who is ready to walk the way that you yourself are and that you prepare for him. Without this light of yours, no gate would be found and no way exist. Without your light, none of your faithful would even attain the slightest degree of holiness. For holiness is for us the encounter of your light with the faith within us, which we have, of course, always received from your light; and you permit us to reflect it together with you. In the center of the city, you have erected the sign of your Son's Cross as the sign of the greatest holiness. And when you let those

[1] These prayers could be characterized more precisely as prayers of the Church on earth: the way they sound before God's throne in heaven. The earthly and heavenly Church is, of course, only one single unity, and on earth it is informed about the Church in heaven through the Apocalypse. On the origin of these prayers, see above, pp. 87–88.

who are yours walk the way of holiness, you bestow this Cross upon them in the measure and manner you like, so that they accept it, carry it, and, together with the Son, bring it back to you, the almighty God. You let your Son, together with your saints, restore to you the Cross that was his, but you also receive it together with the Son so that he sees that you, Father, recognize the face and the work of your Son in every one of your servants. You have given them the holiness that your Son gained for them on the Cross. So that, in perfect love toward you, he might learn that you have accepted his perfect sacrifice, you make the imprint of the Cross visible in the sacrifice attempted by your saints. All of us who receive the message from John about the perfect city want to serve you in new love, with new faith and new hope. We all want to try according to the measure of our failing strength to participate in the work of your Son, so that your glorification by the Son, Father, may also become more visible in us and in all those entrusted to our care in your entire Church. Amen.

2. "THE WALL OF THE CITY HAD TWELVE FOUNDATION STONES ON WHICH WERE WRITTEN THE TWELVE NAMES OF THE TWELVE APOSTLES OF THE LAMB"

It should become clear how the Apostles' Creed opens the twelve gates. It is not as though each article of the Creed were to be attributed to a single apostle or had a special importance for him. But the spirit of grace of the apostles, who all share their missions with each other—because all these missions originate in the one spring of the Lord—opens all twelve gates of the city, so that all twelve articles are proclaimed not only by all the apostles together, but by each in his own particular way. In the prayer is shown how the Apostles' Creed appears in the light of the Holy City; how it can be prayer in the spirit of heaven.

1. *I believe in God, the Father almighty, creator of heaven and earth.* God, holy Father, you created heaven and earth and have filled both of them now with a new light in the vision of John. You have shown him your creation, the way it looks when the light of your Holy City illumines it, and you yourself are this light with which you have filled your City. All things are illuminated by your light; the entire City has become transparent, luminous, sparkling, and fruitful in the holiness bestowed by you. We ask you to make a gift of this same holiness to your entire people, your Church, your priests, to all your believers, all who search for you, to all who seek after truth, as to those who already possess it: for it is the light of your love.

2. *And in Jesus Christ, his only Son, our Lord.* God, Father, you have given us your only Son; he is our Lord. You have given us faith in him so that we may see you through him in the way you yourself deign to reveal yourself to us. We all ask you: Receive in grace our memory, our spirit, our will, so that everything that is in us may be filled by this faith of your light. All of us ask you: Give us the light that you bestow on us in the belief in your Son, so that we may continue to radiate it the way you also gave it to your Son and he continued to bestow it. Grant that our faith in your Son may become such a faith as your perfect light demands.

3. *Who was conceived by the Holy Spirit, born of the Virgin Mary, was crucified, died, and was buried.* Father, you gave us your eternal Son in such a way that his life among us can

be told in words with which any other human life can be described and summarized. But at the beginning, you sent him forth through the Holy Spirit and let him be carried in the Virgin's womb; and she is carrying him now and will give birth to him, just as you beget him eternally and are carrying him in your womb. And because he is born of the Virgin Mary, you allow us all to participate in the mystery of such a birth in the Spirit, and, together with him, you let us grow strong in obedience and wisdom. We ask you to grant that the life of those who are your own, the life of the faithful, may be summed up as simply and clearly as the earthly life of your Son. Let every life to which you have given of your own holiness become what it ought to be so that it might be worthy of the grace that your Son offers it. Let the Holy Spirit participate in our becoming and growing. Grant that, according to your will and for your glorification, the Son may bestow on us a life that may be counted as a life of one of his brothers in you, Father.

4. *He descended into hell.* Beyond his death on the Cross, Father, your Son even let himself be sent into hell, into this most desolate wasteland upon which no living being had set foot. He did it in order to share more fully in all your mysteries, to show you that he will never allow himself to become satisfied in your service, in his love for you. He offered you the going-beyond of the Cross along with this further going-beyond of his descent into hell. Knowing, Father, what your Son has suffered and gone through out of love for you and for our sakes, let us become men who show themselves grateful for this. From the same love that you bestow on your Son in the Holy Spirit, let us try to offer you and him everything that we do and suffer, hope and love, in a way that is agreeable to you. Do not allow the grace of your Son to be lost upon

us. Let the Yes of our answer sound with such force that you can receive it as one that is powerful, irrevocable. You can indeed hear it as such because the overflowing love and grace of your Son, granted to us, has stood security for it, that when our strength is at an end and failing, his own inability to go on is pledged to round out our mere attempt at a true achievement; at *his* achievement, Father, which he offers to you, to your eternal light, by his descent into darkness.

5. *On the third day he rose again from the dead.* Triune God, Father, Son, and Spirit, grant that the Resurrection of your Son from the dead and anew into eternal life may also mean a rebirth of each individual believer, the rebirth of the Church as a whole and, through the Church, of all creation. We who are powerless want to be raised up by the power of this Resurrection in such a way that the grace of the Resurrection may bring about our renunciation of this old life that until now we have called our own. The Lord has visited the dead, and out of their midst he has risen so that all the dead—those already buried and those still dwelling on earth—may have a part in his Resurrection. In rising, he brought the work of the Cross to its ultimate fullness. Allow us, Lord, to be drawn up with him, to dare the attempt to arise from our graves with you, even if this increases the weight of what you have to drag along. Let none of us perish and decay; take us all with you to God. Let us share in the light of your Resurrection, which is found anew in the light of your heavenly temple and which you, together with the Father and the Spirit, grant to the Holy City.

6. *He ascended into heaven and is seated at the right hand of God the Father almighty.* Father, you have again received

your Son, who with your holy consent departed from you in order to become man. And you have given him, who is unique, the place of honor at your right hand. He is enthroned next to you. You are enthroned together in the joy of perfect heavenly reunion in the unity of the Holy Spirit. We ask you: Let your Church share in this joy. Let her never withdraw from your union. Father, grant that your Son may bring to you your whole Church, as she believes in this unity today on earth and as it is beheld and praised in heaven in the Holy City. O Lord, do not consider our infinite distance, all our faults and mistakes that burden us. Rather take us, in virtue of the grace of your holy Church in heaven, in virtue of the grace of all the saints who are our advocates, receive us so that we may eternally rejoice in your countenance and may behold you and your Son enthroned with you in the unity of the Holy Spirit.

7. *To judge the living and the dead.* Father, in the Apocalypse you have permitted us a glimpse into your judgment. You have shown us the glory of your Holy City only after we have witnessed something of the judgment. And, Father, your Son has recorded something for each one of us in his Book of Life. And this was an expression of his love. Acknowledge that this love is truth, and grant that every one of us may reach you. Give us this grace, make us a gift of this light. Even if we stand before your court as great sinners and only in this moment comprehend the depth of our transgressions, still, after your judgment has purified us and your fire has annihilated everything in us that separates us from you, grant that the judgment of your Son's love might receive us and bring us to you. Let this come to be out of the love you have for him, in your own name as in the name of the Son and the Holy Spirit.

8. *I believe in the Holy Spirit.* Father, I believe in the Holy Spirit because you have given him through your Son: you promised him as long ago as the Old Covenant and in holy baptism and confirmation give him anew to each believer. I believe in this Spirit because you sent him to your twelve apostles after your Son had returned to you. When you let him descend at Pentecost, you gave us a new hope in the Spirit. The grace bestowed on us through the coming of the Son from heaven, through his death and Resurrection, did not conclude with his Ascension. In allowing him to send us the Spirit from above, you prove to us that you received your Son, who returned to you with his mission fulfilled, in such a way that henceforth the graces will not cease to descend from heaven to earth. And thus in the Spirit you have made us the gift of a never-ending hope. Father, let it be ours. Let it be ours in such a way that it will become an ever-new faith and remain ready to be confirmed ever anew in the light of your holiness. Give us above all the love of your Spirit, in your name as in the name of the Son and in the name of the Spirit of this love.

9. *One holy catholic Church.* Lord, you have left us your holy Catholic Church as your Bride who would tell us about you, her Bridegroom, and make him come alive in us. Before the Father and the Holy Spirit, in the community of your Mother and all the saints, you profess to be the Bridegroom of this Church. With all of them you are at our disposal in the Church that you founded as an indissoluble union of love for the salvation of the world, which was on the verge of being lost. Thus we thank you, Lord, for the gift of your Church, and may our faith be the expression of this gratitude. Recognize in our faith, even if it is weak and tepid, our gratitude to you and the Father and the Spirit for having given us in the Church

the promise of receiving us into the communal light of your triune love.

10. *The communion of saints.* Father, you have shown us the spouse of the Lamb, the Holy City in heaven. We were allowed to see it so that we might desire to learn ever more about you and be struck more deeply by your light. You have shown her to us in her perfect spotlessness and holiness, as she receives your light without any opacity. We know, Father, that we are sinners and far from having received as much holiness as is necessary to be accepted into your Holy City. But Father, you have given us an image of this City in your Church. And through the faith you give us, you allow us to enter into a community with the true saints and thus, through the power of your faith, to participate now, already, in the holiness of heaven. You also receive every one of us who wants to believe into your holy Church in order to give him a share in your Son's holiness in his Bride. We thank you for this gift; it is a growing gift of your ever-deeper dwelling within us. Grant, Father, that every one of us will be received into this community of love and that each of us will show many others the way into this community. Grant that through your grace this community will continue to increase until it has reached the completeness your Son has won for it on the Cross.

11. *Forgiveness of sins.* Lord, we stand before you as sinners. Were we to look only upon ourselves, our confession would have no end. Everywhere we would recognize our offenses that we have committed in thought, word, and deed. Not only individual sins, but their perpetual intertwining. Lord, for these sins you mounted the Cross, you suffered, died, and descended into hell, to gain the forgiveness of all our sins. And you made it possible for us to tell our sins in holy confession, in humility and contrition,

but also in the certainty of your forgiveness. In confession you forgive us; you forgive us in judgment so that we may come to you, into heaven. Everything that you show us of this heaven, of the triune life, of the City of your saints has thus become a future reality for us. It is reality in heaven, but we will receive a share in it through the forgiveness of sins. And you show us the way to extricate ourselves from our sins: we should look more toward you than toward our sins, should trust more in your grace than we fear from our sins. For your forgiveness is more than merely a wiping away of our guilt; it is fulfilled in seeing you, in the love you give us to pass on to our brothers. Where there was sin, there is now no gaping void; rather, your face is shining there: let us transmit this radiance to everyone around us.

12. *The resurrection of the body, and the life everlasting. Amen.* Just as you, Lord, have risen from the dead and have become newly alive and visible, dwelling among those who are yours, so grant that we also may be resurrected in our flesh. We are allowed to rise as those who we are on earth, provided with the gifts the Father gave us at creation, but purified by your grace, endowed with your communal Holy Spirit. We are allowed to rise, not for a brief moment, comparable to our earthly life, but for an endless, eternal life that is yours, that knows no limitation, and that will be for us participation in your fulfillment, in the eternal love between the Father and you in the Holy Spirit. Amen.

3. THE BOOK OF LIFE OF THE LAMB

Lord, you came into the world as the eternal lamb of the Father to bring all men life. Not only your limited, human life, but your eternal life. In obedience to the Father, you brought your whole life to the world for us, imparted it to us, to each one of us. And for whoever carried a longing for life in his heart, you fulfilled his longing by filling it to the brim and to overflowing with your own life. You lavished your life to that extent so that every one of us might gain a superabundance of life, and this superabundance is the promise of eternal life. And so that no one would be overlooked, so that you could show the Father that you had come to redeem everyone and to give your life for everyone, you entered each of the redeemed in your book. Thus this book has become a sign for the Father that you have forgotten no one, that you wanted to bring everyone home. You not only saved our life on earth, on the Cross; you have also furnished proof of this in heaven.

Lord, teach us to thank you for that. Teach us to consecrate our mortal life to you. May it be spent in your service and show you that we have at least some idea of the extent of your sacrifice, the value of your gift, the superabundance of your lavishness. Indeed, you give us nothing less than eternal life. Teach us to receive your life into ourselves in such a way that our earthly life may already bear witness that we are carrying eternal life within ourselves. We ask you, therefore: do not consider it a sacrifice when we dare to attempt this, take it only as a sign of our love, which indeed originates in you and in the unity in which you live with the Father and the Holy Spirit. Amen.

4. IN THANKSGIVING FOR THE APOCALYPSE

Father, you allowed Saint John an insight into the fullness of your glory. What you showed him of heaven was a part of your splendor. You showed him this so that he would then show it to all of us, as encouragement, as help, as a sign that the promise of eternal life was being realized. You let him see the beginning of this fulfillment. For what he got to see was not a distant promise, but its direct fulfillment. You made him this gift for all of us, so that we might receive a greater, more Christian, ecclesial understanding of your grace and your love. You granted John entrance into your heaven, allowed him to see your angels and the entire community of the Heavenly City. When he later returned to earth, into the loneliness of his Christian life, he knew that you would not leave the lonely one lonely, that you have not forsaken the forsaken one. And he knew that loneliness and forsakenness and temptation are only there to smooth the path of your faithful to your heaven, to let them share in carrying some of what your Son carried for all of us in this life in order to take us along with him, in order to bring this ideal of sharing closer to every one of your faithful. But now, even in loneliness and forsakenness, it has become easier to share the carrying and to take others along because you have revealed to John the purpose and result.

And in everything that you showed of heaven, Father, it had to become clear to us that it has always corresponded to the love that joins you with your Son and the Spirit; that your heaven with its visibility, your eternity with its promises, are only signs of your eternal love into which you have decided to lead us. And in all the angels and in those who accompanied John, you showed that you already supply us on earth with heavenly guardians who have the task of helping us find more easily the gates of your Holy City. In the name of your love, we thank you for your love. Amen.

5. PRAYER OF ADORATION OF THE
SERVANTS BEFORE THE THRONE
OF GOD AND THE LAMB

Lord, we ask you, fill all our prayer with your own word. Let your word so grow in us that when we pronounce it, you can hear it in a way acceptable to you. Do not permit this word to leave us behind; grant that it might take us along. Allow your holy word to lead us perfectly to you, as far as corresponds to your holy will, to have us with you.

Allow us, Lord, to learn to glorify the Father, you, and the Spirit with your strength and your holiness, in the way you expect of us. To that end, let everything in us perish that is not yours. Annihilate it in such a way that it never returns. Let it vanish so completely that you are able to see in us, in each of us believers, only what is yours, what you bestow upon us and what increases in us only through your grace. Grant that we live exclusively for your service in virtue of your word living in us. Grant that everything we do or want or strive for may belong to your service alone. Give us a share in your adoration of the Father. Do not tire of strengthening our weakness—even if it is done by substituting your weakness for ours—so that we may help you to continue your task of glorifying the Father. Make us this gift from the strength that your saints lend us. Make us this gift from the promised strength of heaven fulfilled. Give it to us in view of all that you have suffered for us. Vouchsafe that we may remain faithful and that every breath in us may be filled with your Spirit. Then we would be as we should be according to your design, as you saw us in the will of the Father when you left your heaven to save us.

We ask you for this because your Mother has already asked you for it and because by her life, by accompanying you during your life on earth, she showed how serious she was about her offer. And she showed how seriously we, too, could mean it if we dared to try walking her path in your strength, in following her example of purity and out of gratitude that she brought you to us. Let your Mother supply what is lacking in our prayer. Let her adoration of you move you to give us the spirit of this adoration. We ask you for this in her name and ask you, too, in the name of the Father, in your own name, and in the name of the Holy Spirit. Amen.

6. "THE LORD GOD IS THEIR LIGHT"

Father, from all eternity you possess eternal life, which you now reveal to us in heaven. You show it to us in such a way that we can carry the knowledge of it into our every-day faith; it may accompany our earthly life. But not so that it might make our present existence appear worthless and no longer worth living, but because you allow us already to give away our present life, to place it at your disposal as if in thanksgiving for the eternity you give us. We know that our earthly life was so conceived by you and granted to us that we could have spent it wholly in purity and in grace. We turned away, and you sent your Son to us so that he might change our turning away from you back to a turning toward you. And in doing this, he showed us by his life that a human life is not worthless. And if he himself did not need it to prepare himself for eternal life, all the more did he let it become a preparation for us. Father, your Son had eternal life within himself when he shared our life. He had it so much within himself that, through the grace of his dwelling among us, we obtained proof that we, too, are allowed to carry this eternal life within us. We ask you, Father, grant that our daily life may also become an answer to your eternity. Give us the strength to carry now, already, the weight of your eternity; we do indeed perceive it to be a heavy burden because you have not yet so purified us that we can consider it as pure gift. Our earthly life retains something of expiation, but we want to be grateful to you that your gifts are often difficult to bear. And yet they are so full of grace, so filled with your presence that we joyfully consent to all that you give us; in the knowledge that, for the fulfilling of your promises, our consent can be taken along into eternal life, as it will ultimately be yours in heaven together with your Son and your Spirit. Let us come to you, Father, but by the path you want; give us only the love that your eternity bestows on us every day. Amen.

7. OUR FATHER

Our Father. Father of your Son and Father of all who believe in you and who come to you through the grace of the Son and the Spirit. Father of creation, Father of the Old Covenant, Father of the New Covenant, Father of every one of us. *Who art in heaven.*[2] You are in heaven, are the light of heaven. You are the light of all holiness, the light of faith, the light of hope, the light of love. You are in heaven, where in your triune spirit faith, love, and hope meet in the unity of light, in that unity which makes heaven your heaven. *Hallowed be thy name.* We want to keep your name holy by the holiness that you have

Adrienne's remarks on the Our Father. (These remarks are of interest above all because, dictated in answer to my further questioning, they show how the individual words that perhaps appear plain to us were laden with meaning for Adrienne.)

[2] A parallel between the triune God and the trinity of faith, love, and hope that *become* one unity as Father, Son, and Spirit *are* one. Faith, hope, and love are in God, but from them God fashions his dwelling place, his heaven.

shown us in your light.[3] We want to remain conscious, we want to remind ourselves—daily, forever, and without ceasing—that your name contains in itself all holiness.[4] We want to bow down before this holiness, to guard it as the mystery that binds you with the Son and the Holy Spirit and embraces us all when we behold your light. *Thy kingdom come.* We ask you, let the kingdom of your light come to us in the name of your holiness that we beheld; let it shine in our darkness; let it make days of our nights. Let the grace of your kingdom arise where just a while ago was the bitterness of our sins. Take our earthly life into your eternal one as a sign that you will allow our earth to enter into your heaven in the new form it will receive there.[5] *Thy will be done on earth as it is in heaven.* Father, you, together with the Son and Spirit, have one single, divine, holy, indivisible will. Let it come into being within us just as it has come into being in your heaven of light. Grant that we may fulfill it in the way your Son has shown us it is to be fulfilled.[6] *Give us this day our daily bread.* For

[3] That is the perfect holiness that becomes intelligible to us through God's light and in his light. Had God not shown it to us in his light, had we been forced to imagine it ourselves, it would have appeared to us vastly weakened. But since it was shown in his light, we have a real knowledge of the divine holiness. Even if subsequently the light in us is darkened again, we nevertheless know what it contains in essence since we have seen it in the light of God.

[4] That is to say: the Son's word restores for us the light of God's holiness. The holiness that we see in heaven we have in his word on earth, and now we see God's holiness simultaneously in both.

[5] God allows his kingdom to have come in us to the extent that he allows our life in faith, and so on, to share in eternal life.

[6] It is the will of the Father that, through the Incarnation, received a fulfillment comprehensible and visible to us. Ever since the Son accomplished it day by day and fashioned each day on earth into a vessel of the Father's will, this will is no longer anything abstract for mankind. He shows us in the act of his coming and remaining in his mission how this will is to be fulfilled. The Son himself is in the act and in the state of fulfilling.

each day give us the bread we need to be able to serve you. Give us the bread for our body so that this body may fulfill its appointed task on earth within your will; that already on earth it may prepare for its life in heaven after the resurrection of the flesh; that it may become a tool that enables each of your servants to perform his service as long as you need him here below.[7] *And forgive us our trespasses.* Father, forgive us for these; every time we fall, show us that your Son died for each one of us; let us experience anew in each confession that, after the confession of our sins, we have been received again into the grace of your obedience—the obedience of your Son to you. Forgive us all our trespasses, for your Son surely died for every single one of our sins out of love for you; forgive us these out of the love that unites you with your Son.[8] *As we forgive those who trespass against us.* We ourselves want to learn to forgive; you show us how we should do it by forgiving us who are guilty of the Lord's death. Your forgiveness on the Cross was so great that from it and from the powerlessness left to your Son we have learned in faith how to forgive.[9] *And lead us not into temptation.* For we are weak, Father, who art in heaven; we know how weak we are, how easily we slip. Our stumbling begins with every moment in which we

[7] Daily bread has its unity in the service of God: it is bread for service. Bread of the body, as specified in this prayer: bread of the Spirit as doctrine, prayer, contemplation; and these three are in the unity of service as well, so that the spirit may learn to become fit to serve.

[8] Forgiveness of sins and obedience are most intimately linked. Obedience as the extreme obedience on the Cross and, at the same time, as our obedience in confession: that is what forgives our sins.

[9] We *are* forgiven, in grace and gratuitously. And thus we obtain in forgiveness a surplus power of forgiving that must be lavished on those who trespass against us. This power comes continuously from the Son, who is continuously taking our sins upon himself. In forgiving us and showing us what we must do, he almost forgives already in our place those whom we have to forgive.

forget you, when we no longer fulfill your will in the measure you expect from us. Lead us not into temptation, for you see how very weak our whole assent remains, even if it is made with the strength of our faith. Accept it, nevertheless, as a firm promise because you know, after all, that in virtue of your Son's grace, all of his love is contained in it as well. But let us not frustrate this love of your Son by your leading us into temptation. Do not test our weakness to an extent that would not correspond to your Son's forbearance for us and to the love he has poured into us.[10] *But deliver us from evil. Amen.* Deliver us from everything that is impure, unholy, from everything that would be ours and would withdraw from your light. Illuminate us wholly; make us transparent; in the light of your Son's Cross, make us worthy of the light that you, together with the Spirit, bestow upon the saints. So be it, Father, in your name, in the name of your Son, in the name of your Spirit, and in the name of all your saints. Amen.

8. "I AM THE FIRST AND THE LAST"

Lord, you tell us from heaven that you are the first and the last. Grant us understanding of this word in faith, this word that you speak to us over and over again, that you say again and again, like a confession of love to us and to the Father at the same time. Let us understand the meaning of your word, become the first in our day and remain the first and the last simultaneously until our evening. Occupy the place of the first and the last in each of our thoughts

[10]We are weak because we are sinful. But there exists a parallel between our weakness—which is one of sinfulness—and the powerlessness of the Son, which is a weakness of purity. When the Father does not lead us into temptation, it is because he remembers then how weak purity made the Son on the Cross.

so that everything we think about may become a prayer enveloped in your presence. In so naming yourself, you offer yourself to be our beginning and end. You offer to accomplish all of the work in us, to bring us, worthy of your promises, to the Father. Lord, form us. Form our faith; form our life out of your own being—being that is the beginning and the end. Uproot everything in us that does not begin and end in you, everything that prevents us from following you perfectly. When you are beginning and end in us, your obedience to the Father becomes alive in us. Lord, let our obedience be offered to your will, give us anew each day the strength to receive you as our first and last; just as the Father possesses you in the Spirit as the first and the last, so grant that we may learn from your Father, from you, from your Spirit to possess in you our beginning and end forevermore. Amen.

9. LET HIM WHO HEARS SAY, "COME!"

O Lord, at the origin of all things, God the Father called you: "Come!", and you came. This, his call, which you heard and followed, you also place within us so that it may possess the living power in us to allow you to come in truth. You also allow us to call you: "Come!" And in allowing that, you show us that you will answer this call and will come; that you are coming, that we need only to call you, that we are allowed to ask you. You hear us. You hand this call over to us with all the power of your divine will: you place yourself perfectly at the disposition of this call that you give to us. As if you were the servant and we the ones with power. You reveal your mystery to us in this "Come!", the mystery that consists in your never hearing a question without answering it. You let us call for you, in whatever situation we may be in, and you come.

Lord, grant that every one of us, your whole Church, all who have not yet found the way to you and your Church, may learn—each individual and all together, particularly all those in your Church—to let your call resound. Teach us to say: "Come!" in the same spirit of prayer that you instilled in us when you began to pray among us: Father, your kingdom come! Amen.

FINAL REFLECTIONS

Adrienne von Speyr in This Hour of the Church

The preceding pages make a summary almost unnecessary. It is sufficient to give some indication of the timeliness of Adrienne's mission in the Church's present hour. Into confused and perplexing situations, she brings directions and solutions of penetrating, often painful clarity. But they are directions that all flow from the source-waters of biblical revelation.

God is the truth, and he makes a gift of his truth to man, who is then in the truth only if he lives in God's truth. That means for today: not in introspection, not by individual and social (sociological) psychology does man come to the truth. If applied psychology is authentic, it will help man to get away from himself and become free for God and neighbor. Authentic existential analysis will disclose to man his decadence, his lovelessness, his need for redeeming grace and for following the way he has been shown.

Man is in the truth if, being open himself, he lives in the truth of God that has been opened and given over to him. That is above all the truth of the divine love or of the divine Trinity, which is the same thing. What Paul calls "*en Christô*", existing in the sphere of Christ's being and life, is living with Christ in the triune love, walking with Christ on the paths between Father and Son in the Holy Spirit. With that, every artificially erected barrier between heaven and earth, this life and the life to come, collapses, something that Paul also says expressly: Christ has "made

... both [worlds] one, and has broken down the dividing wall of hostility, by abolishing in his flesh the law of commandments and ordinances" (Eph 2:14–15). It can truly be said that Adrienne von Speyr has demonstrated most convincingly before us the Christian possibility of working actively in a worldly profession and sphere of responsibilities while in undiminished, indeed strengthened and increased, contemplation and the prayer of faith. And she has thereby exposed the conflicting ideologies that frequently circulate today as incorrect and unchristian. It cannot be asserted that as a mystic she had been given an extraordinary grace in this regard. The intense experiences of the truths of the faith that she received as a gift all really went in the direction in which every Christian life must advance, in the realization (in Newman's sense) of the incarnational movement of God, which, however, was a movement of *kenosis*, of a humbling unto death on the Cross. And the God thus humbled is at the same time the exalted one, the one sitting at the right hand of the Father in heaven, and the one who at the same time continues to dwell among us—especially in the Eucharist— until the end of the world.

It is here that an explanation will be found for one aspect in the life and thought of Adrienne von Speyr that must have become painfully conspicuous to many a reader of this book: her animosity toward and decided rejection of the Protestant forms of Christianity from early youth on. While as a child, knowing nothing of Catholicism, she could only say that something was not right, "God is different", she expressed it very clearly once in recent years: "The Protestants miss the ultimate seriousness of the Incarnation, the becoming-flesh. That is why everything often remains so theoretical, speculative." The two main emphases that were important to her later, however, were already established in her youth: in the meeting with Ignatius and in the vision of Mary. For Adrienne, the full import of the Incarnation implied the theological relevance of the relationship of mother and child (wherein all so-called Marian dogmas are implied with compelling logic) and likewise the theological, christological relevance of incarnational Christian obedience, which is possible only through the Catholic understanding of the office of authority. Thirdly, we must add the real presence of the event of the Cross in confession and absolution, the real presence of Christ's flesh and blood in the Eucharist. It seemed totally unacceptable to Adrienne von Speyr to relativize this "Catholic plus" or to go back beyond the position of the Catholic Newman into his Anglican period with his branch theory[1] like many Catholic theologians of today. But one must not overlook the other side: Where in the two-thousand-year-old Catholic tradition of mysticism and spirituality has the Word of God in Holy Scripture been listened to so radically, where has this Word been lived so exclusively as here? Has the true concern of Luther and the Reformation not been taken into the womb of the Church in this unique charism and in fact in such a way that the so-called Catholic excesses—for example, the life of the evangelical counsels—prove to be legitimate, indeed quite central, evangelical concerns arising directly from listening to the Word of God? It is not without reason that Adrienne von Speyr had a very friendly association with Grandchamp (the feminine counterpart of Taizé).

How Does One Read Adrienne von Speyr?

Faced with the quantity of her writings, many are at a loss; they struggle through two or three books, and then, on account of the seeming endlessness, they lose the desire

---

[1] This theory regards the various major Christian Churches as being equal "branches" of a common trunk.

and courage to read further. For these I repeat what I said previously: something that has grown out of slow meditation is also properly absorbed only slowly and meditatively. This is especially true of the commentaries on Scripture; they are best suited as a preparation for one's own contemplative prayer. One reads the verse of Scripture, then Adrienne von Speyr's reflections on it, and uses them as "points of meditation". For example, *Die Bergpredigt* (the Sermon on the Mount), *Passion nach Matthäus* (the Passion according to Matthew), *Dienst der Freude* (Service of Joy), and the *Letter to the Colossians*, *Achtzehn Psalmen* (Eighteen Psalms), and the *Gleichnisse des Herrn* (Parables of the Lord).

A different approach to her work is offered by her smaller, treatise-like works, which develop a special aspect of her theological vision. Before all others, *Handmaid of the Lord* should be read, then works of smaller scope like *The Gates of Eternal Life*, *The Boundless God*, *The Face of the Father*, and similar ones. From this point, the more extensive works like *The World of Prayer* and *Confession* are more easily accessible.

A third approach, which of course requires some knowledge of her writings, would be the systematic search for important theological themes. What, for example, does Adrienne von Speyr have to say about the place of charisms in the Church? This is to be found of course in the commentary on 1 Corinthians 14 (in connection with chapters 12 and 13). What is her view on the apocalyptic vision (see the beginning of the commentary on the Apocalypse)? What about the connection of office and love in the Church (see John, chapters 20 and 21)? This approach will be facilitated by the publication of the posthumous volumes (particularly vols. 5 and 6) and by an index.